WOMEN OF THE
COVENANT

SPIRITUAL WISDOM *from* WOMEN *of the* BIBLE

WOMEN OF THE COVENANT

SPIRITUAL WISDOM *from* WOMEN *of the* BIBLE

KIMBERLY SOWELL
EDNA ELLISON

NEW HOPE
PUBLISHERS

Birmingham, Alabama

New Hope® Publishers
P. O. Box 12065
Birmingham, AL 35202-2065
www.newhopepublishers.com

New Hope Publishers is a division of WMU®.

Library of Congress Cataloging-in-Publication Data

Sowell, Kimberly.
 Women of the covenant : spiritual wisdom from women of the Bible : ten
studies for individuals or groups : including a leader's guide for group
study facilitators / Kimberly Sowell and Edna Ellison.
    p. cm.
 ISBN 978-1-59669-270-1 (sc)
 1. Women in the Bible--Textbooks. 2. Christian women--Religious
life--Textbooks. I. Ellison, Edna. II. Title.
 BS575.S535 2009
 220.9'2082--dc22
                              2009003261

ISBN-10: 1-59669-270-7
ISBN-13: 978-1-59669-270-1

N094151• 0609 • 4M1

DEDICATION

Not one word of worth flows from me except it comes from the
creative inspiration and fountain of wisdom that is my God.
Thank you, my Savior and Lord!

—Kimberly Sowell and Edna Ellison

TABLE OF CONTENTS

WELCOME

od's women...that's what we are. From the beginning of Creation, God has called women to love Him, long for Him, and honor Him in their lives. It is our privilege to offer you this little Bible study, which we hope you'll find helpful as you grow closer in your walk with Him.

The book features true stories of ten amazing, godly, strong—yet very human—women of the Word: Abigail, Rebekah, Miriam, Naomi, Hannah, Phoebe, a needy widow, the mother of King Lemuel, a generous widow, and Rahab. We have found them good examples, teaching all of us how to avoid sin and model courage. They have inspired us, and we hope they will inspire you as you search for answers to life's challenges.

Throughout each chapter, we have included study questions that may be used for your private study or a group study, each person responding as she desires—whether in an individual time with God, reaching out for encouragement and intimacy with Him, or perhaps sharing in a group of women who encourage each other and grow in corporate worship as well as friendship. **"Going Deeper"** questions drive readers to study the Scriptures in more depth. **"Personal Reflections"** questions are designed to spur readers to introspection, prayer, and meditation. You'll find also some **"Fast Facts"** that provide interesting information or context from history or today. And we also encourage you to interact with **"Just for Fun"** by making some practical application to your life. Finally, **"Heart Connections"** provide an insight into our personal spiritual journey.

May you be challenged to live your own life as a woman of the covenant by examining the lives of these great women of the Bible.

CHAPTER ONE

ABIGAIL:

GODLY ROSE AMONG THE THORNS

By Kimberly Sowell

During a Bible study on heaven, one of the women became very distressed. She couldn't imagine living in heaven without her beloved groom as her husband. My response was an easy one: "Consider all of the other wives from the beginning of time; heaven wouldn't be so grand for many of them if they had to remain married to their earthly husbands for eternity!"

Have you ever met a precious, gentle-spirited woman who was married to a brash, hard-to-get-along-with man? Most of us have met "the odd couple" before, and we wonder: *How did she end up with him?* During Bible times, when marriages were arranged, such mismatches seem easier to understand. Imagine the patience needed by many a God-fearing woman as she endured life with her lazy Larry or grouchy Gus.

One such woman of endurance was Abigail, wife of Nabal. As you study her life experiences, try to find ways to relate her life lessons to your own situation today. You are called to bear with difficult people who can sometimes create trying circumstances for you, whether it be your husband, children, or even your brothers and sisters in the family of God. Your walk with Christ can thrive despite the chaos around you. What are the marks of godliness we see in Abigail's life?

Godliness Isn't a Product of Environment
(1 Samuel 25:2-3)

The evidence from Scripture is clear—Abigail was not like her husband. Her name means "father rejoices," but Nabal surely brought shame to his family with his evil ways. While they shared a household, they did not share guiding life principles.

The world is full of excuses for bad behavior. "My mother was a poor example." "All of my co-workers curse." "My friends talked me into it." Abigail is a stellar example that the old adage is *not* true—we are not destined to be a product of our environments.

The behaviors and attitudes of the people around us can certainly have an influence on our choices. Godly people can inspire us to honor God and embrace the Christian life, and wise people can help us to increase in wisdom (Proverbs 13:20). However, those who despise good can entice us to follow a crooked path.

Fast Fact

The name Nabal means "fool."

Going Deeper

What do the following Scriptures teach us about evil associations?

- Ecclesiastes 9:18

- Proverbs 22:24–25

- Romans 14:13

- Matthew 16:23

- Proverbs 4:14–19

God desires us to pursue close relationships with people who will encourage us on our journey for Christ, but some relationships are thrust upon us, such as parents, co-workers, and perhaps in Abigail's case, a foolish husband. A woman of lesser resolve may have chosen to adopt her husband's evil ways, believing that a harsh attitude would be her only means to survive in that household, but God favors the righteous. Proverbs 8:32 instructs, *"Now therefore, listen to me, my children, for blessed are those who keep my ways."* We don't have to stoop to immoral behavior to prosper in the workplace, nor do we have to continue the cycle of poor judgments we may have witnessed from our parents. We can make our own choices, and we will be held accountable for those decisions whether we were consciously considering our ways or simply following the crowd.

Personal Reflections

What excuses have you made for choosing to sin?

GODLINESS CREATES A PERSONAL REPUTATION
(1 SAMUEL 25:4-17)

Nabal proved to be selfish and ungrateful. David and his men had provided protection to Nabal's shepherds, and now David was asking for an act of kindness from a man who should've been glad for the opportunity to return the blessing. David's appeal for a meal was a reasonable request in an era when hospitality was highly valued, yet Nabal carelessly dismissed David and his men. He insulted David, filing him in the category of potential runaway slave and in no way acknowledging his anointing to be king or his valor as a man of God. Nabal denied his debt of gratitude and sent David's men away with a nasty tongue-lashing ringing in their ears.

Nabal's shepherds and servants were likely not surprised to hear of Nabal's poor behavior. Who could they turn to? Nabal was a man who wouldn't listen to reason, labeled as a "son of Belial" (v. 17 KJV). (This is the same label used in the King James to describe the perverted men of Gibeah in Judges 19:22 and the corrupt sons of Eli in 1 Samuel 2:12. Belial is synonymous with Satan in 2 Corinthians 6:15.) Instead of turning to Nabal, they turned to Abigail.

Abigail must have proven herself to be noble and dependable to the servants, for they knew they could present this serious situation to her without fear that she would side with her husband and have them punished for questioning his authority. Her reputation stood apart from that of Nabal, and she was the bright spot of the household, a rose among thorns. God calls us to be holy, set apart, and Abigail is a shining example of a heart resolved to be holy as God is holy.

Personal Reflections

Is there anyone you've been quick to judge because of the family she comes from, the place where she works, or the country or culture she was born into?

Do you fear being looked down upon because of an association you have? How does Abigail's example encourage you?

In what setting do you find it most difficult to be a godly influence? Why?

The servant said to Abigail, *"Know and consider what you will do"* (1 Samuel 25:17). Because of the personal reputation she had built with the servants, they knew they could depend on her. The household was counting on her to do the right thing.

Godliness Takes Action (1 Samuel 25:18-22)

With many lives at stake, Abigail sprang into motion. Not only did she do what her husband should have done in the first place—provide food for David and his men—but she also took extra measures to get involved personally.

David was an anointed man of God, but he was also just a man. His anger was aroused within him, and though he wouldn't take the life of his enemy King Saul, he was ready to annihilate Nabal and his entire household out of revenge. Abigail didn't pretend that food was going to patch up the damage done by Nabal's disrespect, nor did she place the responsibility of diplomacy upon a servant. She mounted up and went out to meet the man who would be king, knowing he was traveling swiftly toward her with sword in hand. She decided to throw herself at the mercy of God by going to David for forgiveness rather than become a victim of her husband's wickedness.

It's not uncommon to find ourselves in the midst of a circumstance created by others' poor behavior. Scandals, church fights, and family feuds are within arm's reach of any of us, and at these pivotal moments in time, we must decide how we will respond. The household of faith is counting on us to do the right thing. Whether we join the fray in our own sin or keep a safe distance in silent apathy; whether we defend the bad behavior of others because of the alliances we have or we shy away because we fear the reflection these behaviors have on our own character—we're pouring water on the grease fire. Prepare to be scorched by the flames!

I know what I would've been tempted to do if I had been Abigail: I'd have tried to change that man by my own will whether he liked it or not. How do I know? Because I've been guilty of it in my own life. Every husband has a little "Nabal" in him, and my wonderful Christian husband is no different. In the early stages of our relationship, I kept a detailed record of the many habits I wanted him to break, and one such habit was his messy variety of housekeeping. He was borderline addicted to his Nintendo when we were young, and I just *knew* he would find more time to house-clean if he weren't so preoccupied with his toy. One day I decided to hide it in a place where he would never find it: his clothes dryer! When he realized what I'd done, I had never seen him angrier than when he tore through each room looking for his video game system. His fury was not from a desire to play the games, but at that moment, he was furious that I was trying forcibly to change his behavior.

∞ JUST FOR FUN ∞

What is an annoying habit that drives you crazy?
What is one of your annoying habits
that drives other people nuts?

Abigail was a wise woman not to try to forcibly mold her husband into a better man. Peter instructed, "*Wives, likewise, be submissive to your own husbands, that even if some do not obey the word, they, without a word, may be won by the conduct of their wives, when they observe your chaste conduct accompanied by fear*" (1 Peter 3:1–2). Trying to change other people—co-workers, friends, and family—is no less precarious. We can encourage, share Scripture, pray for, and be an example to others, but only God can transform their hearts. Abigail knew she couldn't convince her husband to act honorably toward David, but she knew that she could choose to do what would mend the wound of David and honor the Lord.

Personal Reflections

What men and women in Scripture do you admire for taking action?

GODLINESS IS HUMBLE (1 SAMUEL 25:23-35)

The words out of Abigail's mouth confirm her pure motivation for approaching David: *"On me, my lord, on me let this iniquity be!"* she said, and then later, *"Please forgive the trespass of your maidservant"* (vv. 24, 28). She was not there to save her own skin. She did not say: "Please don't harm the servants or me because we're innocent victims, but do whatever you please to Nabal!" She did not have complaining or blaming as her goal: "This is just the sort of behavior I have to put up with all the time. This is entirely Nabal's fault." She had no selfish motive to be relieved of her marital duties to Nabal by the swift sword of a capable warrior: "You'll find Nabal sleeping in the third bedchamber on the left wing of the house. Be careful, he keeps a knife under his pillow, and good luck!" Instead, she explained the facts to David, and she was willing to take the iniquity upon herself. She came only as the humble representative of her household, pleading for mercy at David's feet.

Pride will escalate a conflict, but humility can bring healing to the rip in a relationship. *"A word fitly spoken is like apples of gold in settings of silver"* (Proverbs 25:11). Abigail's wise summation and humble approach caused David to take pause and consider her counsel to avoid bloodshed.

"A man's pride will bring him low, but the humble in spirit will retain honor" (Proverbs 29:23). Though Abigail was the one on her face in the dirt, David thanked God for her, called her blessed, and gladly conceded that he had *"heeded* [her] *voice and respected* [her] *person"* (v. 35).

Going Deeper

Read Proverbs 18:12. Now consider a strained relationship you're experiencing. Ask God to create a sense of humility within you, desiring to humbly approach your adversary because you want ultimately to be humble before God. Spend time praying about how God would have you display a humble spirit and resist the temptation to "save face" or draw boundaries on how far you're willing to go to obey God in humility.

GODLINESS SEEKS PEACE (1 SAMUEL 25:36-37)

When Abigail returned from her journey, which averted a household massacre instigated by her wicked husband, she found said husband feasting like a king and giddy with wine. Nabal was greatly out of touch with reality. However, our heroine passed the test in what might've been the most difficult challenge of all: she held her tongue. Seeing she would get nothing accomplished with a drunkard, she delayed her conversation for the next morning.

Oh, how I've wished my email box had an undo button for the many times I've written someone in haste late at night, only to have a clearer vision of God's hand in the situation by morning. I also admit I've sometimes been in the midst of a difficult conversation with someone when suddenly an unkind or unnecessarily hurtful comment comes into my mind. I sense the Holy Spirit putting a guard over my mouth and I think: *No matter what, I'm not going to say that. It won't help and I don't need to get in that extra dig.* Then the person delivers a low blow or throws one too many punches, and my resolve to be godly gives way to my desire to retaliate. Then there have been those times when my husband has unknowingly started irritating me, and try as I might to hold my tongue until a more appropriate time, my resolve melts like butter and I throw a verbal grenade, deciding that he has delivered the last straw. What's the matter with me?

∽ JUST FOR FUN ∾

Tell on yourself! Name a time when you should've held your tongue but instead blurted out your feelings and created a messy situation.

Can you relate? The tongue is an unruly evil that is untamable (James 3:8). Jesus is our perfect example, knowing there is a time to speak and a time to be silent (Ecclesiastes 3:7). *"He was oppressed and He was afflicted, yet He opened not His mouth; He was led as a lamb to the slaughter, and as a sheep before its shearers is silent, so He opened not His mouth"* (Isaiah 53:7). He paid the price for our sins and honored the will of His Father.

Going Deeper

Read Proverbs 18:2. How does knowing God help us hold our tongues against those who have wronged us?

Read Proverbs 29:11. Describe a time when you regret venting your feelings. How did your loose conversation worsen the situation?

How can a Christian discern whether she is confronting a friend in Christian love or venting her feelings for her own satisfaction?

GODLINESS PREVAILS (1 SAMUEL 25:36-42)

Abigail became the widow of a wicked and foolish man and subsequently the wife of the king of Israel. Her swift and humble actions were the instruments of God to restrain David from committing an evil act of revenge. She did what she could to impact the situation, and God did what only He could to avenge David and bless Abigail.

Personal Reflections

What aspect of godliness do you desire for God to stir up in you? Pray about how God is intervening in your life even now to teach you to be a godly woman in your relationships with others.

Have you poorly handled a conflict in the past? Consider writing a letter to the person involved, humbly asking forgiveness. Avoid the temptation to point out where he or she is also guilty of wronging you. Keep a pure motive to ask for forgiveness in humility before the Lord.

PRAYER MOMENT

Father, I want to be the influencer, not the influenced. I want to be more like Jesus, not more like the people around me who don't know You. Teach me Your ways, Lord. Help me to rise above circumstances and confusion. In Jesus's name, amen.

CHANGE OF HEART

I couldn't wait to tell my husband the good news — God wanted me to quit my job! This decision would allow me to attend seminary, which was three hours away. Kevin and I began to pray about the decision. In the car one day on our way for a campus visit, Kevin said: "Dear, I don't know about this. It's a long drive up here, this is going to be a big expense, and you don't even know what you're going to do with this degree! I'm just telling you this up front, because I don't want you to be disappointed."

I think the teeth marks are still visible where I bit my tongue. My precious husband and had experienced this same scenario many times before: I get excited about something, I share it with him, he doesn't respond with many words, I assume he's in favor, and then he shares his concerns at the moment of decision. More than once I had exploded in anger and resentment when Kevin delivered the bad news at what I considered the last minute, but I purposed in my heart to stay silent. I knew my words would only worsen the situation.

"Lord," I prayed silently, *"I don't have the words to convince my husband that this is Your will. I can't do this without his blessing, either. You're the One who will have to change his mind. If you brought me to the point of being willing to quit my job and go to seminary (it still sounds a little crazy to me too!), then You can speak to his heart as well."*

At the end of the campus visit, my husband turned to me in the counselor's office and said, "This is exactly where God wants you to be. If this is what you want to do, I will support you."

God had spoken to my husband's heart with words that I could not have expressed, and He confirmed His truth to give Kevin peace. Praise God, He is always on time!

PRAYER & PRAISE JOURNAL

Chapter Two

Rebekah:

Lessons in Divine Destiny

By Kimberly Sowell

My daughter always seems to be at the right place at the right time. When we go to children's events, she always gets picked to be the ring-master's assistant or the volunteer from the audience who gets to dance with a penguin. Today she was selected along with only one other child in her school to win a giant stuffed panda bear. How does she do it?

Some call it fate, others call it luck, but we'll call it divine destiny. God directs our paths to guide us into His divine will for our lives. As we read Rebekah's story, we learn what happens when we gracefully fall into God's will, and, conversely, what happens when we try to push our way into God's will.

Prepared to Meet Her Match (Genesis 24:1-28)

When he arrived in Nahor in Mesopotamia, Abraham's most senior servant asked God for very specific clues to find the proper bride for Isaac. Meanwhile, Rebekah arrived before he even finished breathing his prayer. As she strolled up to the well, Abraham's servant didn't know yet that she was the one, but God did. God was at work before the servant ever thought to pray, when He prompted Rebekah to go to the well at just the right time. On the servant's part, her timing was an answer to prayer; on Rebekah's part, it seemed only to be an ordinary moment in the day, until her future unfolded before her that evening.

She was beautiful to behold. As young Rebekah prepared to face the world that morning, what had been her beauty regimen?

Had she brushed her hair until it was full of sheen, pinched her cheeks for a natural blush, or smoothed her skin with aloe? For certain, her preparations were of greater depth than enhancing her physical beauty. Rebekah had been preparing all her life for that God-ordained day, and it was her inner beauty that made her attractive to the servant of Abraham.

Perhaps Rebekah had been praying for a husband, or maybe she was disinterested in the subject of marriage at the time. In any case, she could hardly have imagined that God was molding and shaping her in character and spiritual strength to be an important member of the Hebrew lineage from which would come the Messiah. As she went about her days with the sort of sweet spirit that would prompt a young girl to offer water to an old man and his ten thirsty camels, she was preparing for the greatest adventure of her life.

FAST FACT

A camel can drink up to 40 gallons of water at a time. Watering ten camels, what a tiring chore for Rebekah!

It's in our daily faithfulness to God that we prepare for the exciting journeys of the Christian life. Do not miss that Abraham's servant asked to observe in Isaac's future bride a generous and thoughtful heart and a willingness to serve above and beyond the minimal requirements of social etiquette. For Rebekah, God had afforded her the exact means to develop this beautiful spirit of graciousness, which made her an attractive bridal candidate to the servant. To those who will be challenged to move mountains, God will give the opportunity to build strong spiritual muscles. To those who will stand in the face of persecution and danger, God will give the opportunity to learn courage and endurance. Are you taking full advantage of the opportunities God is giving you to grow spiritually in preparation for the journey ahead?

Personal Reflections

What spiritual traits has God been developing in you? (For example, has He taught you something about wisdom or patience? Has He helped you learn how to deal with difficult peers?)

Can you name a time when you knew God had prepared you to face a situation?

The servant was praying for God to help him find the woman who would be Isaac's wife, and likely Abraham was at home also praying for his future daughter-in-law. These three men—Abraham, Isaac, and the servant—were counting on God, and they were also counting on Rebekah to be the woman who could fulfill the role of godly wife and mother.

You never know when you are the answer to someone else's prayer. Moms and dads are on their knees praying that someone will be able to reach their wayward children. Could you be the answer to that prayer? A lonely single mom is crying out to God for a friend who understands. Could you be that friend? A sister on the other side of the country is praying that a Christian will share the gospel with her lost brother who has shut her out. Could you be the person who will fulfill that request? You may never know how many times you have obeyed the Lord and thus been the answer to someone else's prayer. What an exciting realization that can motivate you to live carefully before the Lord! As you serve and obey God, people are counting on you.

Conversely, are you praying for someone to minister to you or to someone you love? Pray for that person to sense God nudging her, and pray for her to have wisdom and courage to obey.

Moving Forward (Genesis 24:29-58)

What a great night of partying took place in celebration of the engagement of Rebekah to Isaac! However, with the rising of the morning sun came a tense moment in this newly developing relationship—Abraham's servant wanted Rebekah to pack up and leave for the distant land of Hebron *that day*. We can understand the reluctance of Laban and Bethuel, who had hardly met this servant. They had been given no time to absorb the idea of bidding their Rebekah farewell, and they naturally would desire to celebrate her impending marriage with family and friends. Bethuel probably had many father-daughter talks that he had not yet shared with his daughter.

∞ JUST FOR FUN ∞

Hebron was at least one month's journey on camel from Mesopotamia, where Rebekah was raised. How far away would you be willing to move for your Prince Charming?

Despite their reluctance, Laban and Bethuel showed great respect for Rebekah's maturity as they handed the decision over to her. Though she, too, might have had dreams of celebrations and last-minute quiet conversations alone with the family, Rebekah was able to go. She moved forward into her future, placing her trust in God.

Do you catch yourself hesitating as you try to muster the courage to step into the unknown? Consider Rebekah's courageous decision. In her culture, it was very unlikely she had ever been away from home before. For less than a day she had known the servant who would guide her on this journey that would take her far away from home. She was about to become a wife, when just

Women of the Covenant

yesterday she had no knowledge that Isaac even existed. Was he kind? Handsome? Violent? Foolish? Rebekah had seen God's unmistakable hand in the arrangement of this marriage, and with that one piece of knowledge, she was willing to move forward.

Personal Reflections

Fill in the blanks to personalize this statement: I would

be willing to do _____

(an action requiring faith on your part)

if I only knew that God would_____.

(the assurance you seek from God)

No Compromises (Genesis 24:59-67)

Rebekah must have been imagining her husband every day of that long journey. As she looked across the fields at sunset on that sacred wedding night, she saw her beloved coming toward her. He was so close she could almost feel the touch of this man she had longed to embrace for so many days. Yet with a modesty that shielded her fluttering heart, she dismounted her camel to take a more appropriate stance (it's hard to be ladylike on a camel's back!) and she veiled herself in preparation to meet her groom. Rebekah knew it was God's will for her and Isaac to be married, but she wanted to take each step properly and with honor.

The marriage of Isaac and Rebekah is a symbolic representation of our relationship with Jesus Christ. We are the bride of Christ. Just as the father, Abraham, arranged the marriage for his son, the Heavenly Father has arranged our union with our groom, Jesus (Matthew 22:2). The groom's family extended the proposal of marriage, but Rebekah ultimately had to say yes and agree to go; likewise, Christ has offered us a relationship with Him that will last an eternity, but we must accept His proposal.

We can also relate to one other character in this love story: the servant. The master Abraham sent the servant to find a bride for his groom, and we are also sent into this world by our Master to find those who are not yet the bride of Christ, the lost who need a Savior. The servant was willing, prayerful, and speedy in his completion of his assignment. He also made no compromises with respect to his master's expectations and requirements. May we also be such loyal servants.

Going Deeper

Read Ephesians 5:22–33 and list at least five things Christ does for us, His bride.

Meditate on 2 Corinthians 5:9–11. How does the passage relate to how the servant carried out Abraham's instructions? How does the passage relate to how we conduct ourselves as the bride of Christ?

Taking Matters into Her Own Hands
(Genesis 25:19-28; 27:1-17)

It was too bad that Sarah was not alive to mentor her daughter-in-law, because they had a commonality that was painful to bear: infertility. Rebekah and Isaac had been married 20 years before she was able to give birth.

Rebekah was a discerning and spiritually strong woman. She sensed that her pregnancy was not normal, and she turned to God for an answer. What He said was a startling revelation, because in her womb were the fathers of two nations who would strive against one another.

Though customs of that day would have dictated that the oldest twin Esau would one day be the leader of the household and the recipient of the greater portion of Isaac's fortunes, God had ordained for the younger twin Jacob to hold those honors. How could that happen? Did Rebekah gaze up into the stars some nights and wonder how God's prophecy, *"The older shall serve the younger"* (25:23) could ever be fulfilled? She favored Jacob, but knew her husband favored Esau (25:28). And so somewhere along the pathway of rearing these two sons, this woman of prayer and faith unwisely decided she would have to take matters into her own hands.

God's timing is perfect. Rebekah should have learned that from the unmistakable God-ordained circumstances through which Abraham's servant found her at the well. The arrival of her long-awaited twin sons was evidence that God keeps His promises. Despite these personal experiences with God, years later as Isaac was old and ill, Rebekah probably got panicky. She feared Isaac would bless Esau instead of Jacob, so she engineered some trickery to secure his blessing on her favored son.

What causes us to get panicky? Why do we sometimes struggle to wait upon the Lord? A lack of faith is one likely cause; we feel

Fast Fact

Esau's descendants contended with Jacob's descendents when the Israelites were on their exodus from Egypt (Numbers 20:14–21), and they also had skirmishes with Saul, David, and other kings of Israel (for instance, 2 Samuel 8:14; 2 Kings 8:20–22).

more at ease when we can see without a doubt how God has connected the dots to bring good to us. Impatience might be another reason, because we feel we cannot rest in our spirits until we've witnessed the resolution of our stressful situations. Our challenge is to apply our knowledge of God to each personal trial and to rest in knowing that sovereign God is trustworthy.

Personal Reflections

Are you feeling anxious about a situation? Would you feel more or less anxious about it if you knew you were in control of the situation? How does knowing God is in control help to alleviate your anxiety?

Because Rebekah would not wait on God, she manipulated the situation and tried to force the fulfillment of God's prophecy. Her actions were essentially saying, "God, You are going to make Jacob the head over Esau, and You are going to work it out now!" It was God's prophecy, His idea, and thus it should have come at His timing, but Rebekah had made it her personal cause. She schemed the entire deception, and she wanted to force it to happen in her own timing. What's more, this mother who had raised her son to fear the Lord had now taught him how to manipulate others for his own good, a crooked principle he carried with him into adulthood (Genesis 30:25–43).

Losing in the End (Genesis 27:41-46)

When we sin, we can expect to pay consequences. Esau's hatred of Jacob turned murderous, and Rebekah had to live with the knowledge that she had driven this wedge between her rival sons. She had caused heavy grief to come upon her aged husband Isaac. She had deeply wounded her son Esau. And perhaps hardest for Rebekah to bear, she was forced to send her dearly loved Jacob away to protect him from Esau, never to see him again. Rebekah was the loser in the end, and all of her family with her.

Going Deeper

You've probably heard it said, "You're only hurting your-self." God has said, *"He who sins against me wrongs his own soul"* (Proverbs 8:36). What testimony could you share that demonstrates this truth?

Obeying God even when circumstances don't seem to be going your way can be such a struggle. How do these verses encourage you to stay above reproach regardless of the situation? What are the effects of sin?

* Psalm 107:17

* Proverbs 13:15

* Isaiah 57:20

When we don't do things God's way, we cause harm. Even doing the right things for the wrong reasons or in the wrong ways causes sorrow in the end. Rebekah is mentioned in Scripture for many admirable qualities, but she was not consistent when it came to her favorite son. Of course, we are not consistent at all times either, especially when we're passionate about something or someone, as Rebekah was about Jacob. May we learn never to allow worldly passions to drive us, but rather, may we drive our passions as we submit them to the authority of Christ.

PRAYER MOMENT

Heavenly Father, You are trustworthy in all things. I believe Your plan for me is wonderful, and You will bring to pass all that You desire to pour into my life. I desire to be patient and obedient to You. In my times of desperation, please teach me to be still and know that You are God. In Jesus's name, amen.

Heart Connections

WHAT A TRADE!

It was one of those moments you look back on and ask, "What was I thinking?!" My family had moved to South Carolina just a year and a half earlier; I wasn't very popular; I didn't know many people—so why did I feel like I should run for senior class vice president? What *was* I thinking? Well, it was nearly the last day for rising high school seniors to sign up to run for office, and no one had agreed to run for vice president. Thinking I would run unopposed, I took my chances. Little did I know that two more names would go on the ballot before the deadline, which meant I actually had to campaign for a position that I suddenly wasn't sure I wanted.

I had probably the most ridiculous campaign slogan ever devised. I stapled empty Ore-Ida bags to posters and wrote: "It's Ore-Ida to vote for Kimberly." (Right now you're either laughing at me or completely dumb-founded, but have mercy—I was only 17.) As you probably already guessed, my campaign went down in defeat.

At my high school, senior class officers spent the last period of each day doing their civic duties. Once I realized I would have nothing to do that last period (thanks to being a loser!), I signed up at the last minute for yearbook staff. I had never thought about working on the yearbook before but figured it would be a fun way to spend my senior year.

During that last period of each day, a certain 18-year-old boy who was one of the previous year's editors would often stop in to help us with our computer work. His name was Kevin Sowell, my future husband.

Like Rebekah, God had me at the right place at the right time to connect with His preferred future for my life. I might have lost an election, but I gained the best husband I could have ever dreamed of—what a trade! Rebekah and I would tell you that the moral of our stories is this: Every day, no matter what, be the very best you can be for Christ—you never know when God will send an unexpected blessing your way!

PRAYER & PRAISE JOURNAL

CHAPTER THREE

MIRIAM:

SISTER SUPPORT

By Kimberly Sowell

As a child growing up with three brothers and sisters, I monitored my siblings' ratios of treats to chores to ensure fairness. I didn't necessarily care to have more candies than my sister, but I certainly would not settle for less than what she had been given. And I knew I was expected to do chores around the house, but I certainly didn't want to be slaving in the yard if my brother was reclining on the couch with a bag of corn chips.

I see this same doggedness for equality in my middle son, Jay. He doesn't have to be the center of attention, but if he notices his daddy doting on his younger brother or older sister, Jay will suddenly appear and demand the same level of attention and praise. If his brother is singing, Jay will begin singing in a loud booming voice. If his sister is dancing, Jay will dance with all his might, shaking every cell in rhythm from head to toe. "Look, Mommy! Look at me!" he demands. If anyone is getting attention or praise, he wants in the mix. Sibling rivalry!

∽ JUST FOR FUN ∽

Tell about a time when you "demanded"
fair treatment as a child in your home.

Miriam was given the amazing opportunity to experience the miraculous deliverance of God's chosen people from Egypt as a sibling of Moses and member of the inner circle of leadership. Few people are named in that journey to the Promised Land, and even fewer of the named are women. Perhaps in a sense she was a trailblazer for women's leadership in ministry, and we have much we can learn from her finer moments as well as from her mistakes.

Living in Perilous Times (Exodus 1:1-22)

To understand the childhood of Miriam, we must realize the lifestyle of her family and her people. Joseph, son of Jacob, had risen to second in command in the land of Egypt, and his 11 brothers and their families had moved into the land because of the famine. Joseph died and years later a new king sat on the throne of Egypt, one who had not known or loved Joseph. The new king feared and thus oppressed the Hebrews, who had grown great in number and prospered in the land. He made them slaves and treated them harshly. He feared them all the more because they prospered even under duress and affliction; he demanded their baby boys be killed in order to weaken their population in Egypt.

Miriam lived in perilous times for her people. It's likely that every friend and neighbor anticipated the birth of each child with fear and dread, knowing that precious infant boys were being tossed into the Nile. Shrieks and wailing heard in the streets would send a shiver down the spine of every Hebrew woman as she knew that one of her sisters was experiencing the cruel, heartless ripping of her baby boy from her arms, to be thrown into the waters of death. Even a young girl like Miriam could sense the looming darkness of death and oppression.

We also are living in perilous times. Brothers and sisters in Christ are suffering persecution across the world, including legal restrictions, harassment, imprisonment, beatings,

Fast Fact

More than 200 million Christians face serious persecution each day. See the article at http://www .floridabaptistwitness. com/8027.article for more information about their plight.

torture, and even death. Martyrdom for Christ's sake is a twenty-first-century reality that must be faced by many. In other places, particularly the West, while physical persecution may be limited, the spirit of the age is anti-Christ. God is questioned or denied, the Bible is attacked as unreliable, the church is criticized and condemned, and even the concepts of truth and morality are under attack.

Yet in a time when oppression is on the rise and enemies of the Cross are gaining power, God's people are uniting and moving forward to prosper for His kingdom. Missionaries are positioning themselves in regions where the gospel has not been. Bibles are being translated into the heart languages of people who have never read about Jesus before. As earthquakes, famines, and other

Going Deeper

What does Paul tell Timothy in 2 Timothy 3:1–13 about the marks of these perilous last days before the return of Christ?

Read over Paul's description several times. Which of these indicators do you witness most often? Are you guilty of any of these sinful attitudes or behaviors?

Read 2 Timothy 3:14–15; 4:1–5. What does Paul instruct Timothy to do in response to the marks of the perilous times? What is God telling you to do in response to these perilous times?

natural disasters hit nations filled with spiritual darkness, Christians are stepping up to feed the hungry, shelter the homeless, and mend broken hearts with the healing salve that is Jesus Christ. God's people can and do thrive under oppression.

A Discerning Presence (Exodus 2:1-10)

Miriam was a young girl in this scene, the oldest of the three children of the father Amram and the mother Jochebed. Hiding an infant for three months must have been incredibly difficult for Jochebed, and perhaps Miriam assisted with Moses and his brother Aaron, who was three years older than Moses (Exodus 7:7). When the time came for Jochebed to fully surrender her infant Moses into the arms of God by placing him in an ark by the river's side, Miriam desired to be present. She was curious and brave to stand watch over the fate of baby Moses, not knowing if she would witness his deliverance or see his death from any number of possible dangers.

When Pharaoh's daughter had compassion on Moses, Miriam courageously appeared before the princess and spoke up on behalf of her young brother. With her quick thinking and bold notion to step out, she allowed her family to remain intact for a season longer, with Jochebed being paid to nurse and care for her own son.

If Miriam had only stood watch as a casual observer, we might think of her as the rubberneck who strains to see the wreckage while passing by the scene of an accident. But she was not standing her post to be nosy. She was ready to step into the light when she saw an opportunity to benefit her family in the situation.

We watch the lives of others each day. We are more than casual observers with family and friends whom we love and desire to see succeed, but we also take note of those whom we know at a distance. We notice when the office assistant on another floor is often sitting quietly in the break room, seeming alone and depressed. Will we sit with her and allow her to share her burdens with us? We scan a Web site and read about starvation in Zimbabwe. Will we give generously to provide food for the people in need and to open doors for the gospel to spread through Christian relief workers? Or will we be casual observers?

Personal Reflections

What are the needs you have observed lately among people in your sphere of influence?

How are you exposing yourself to the physical and spiritual needs of people around the world?

What would hinder you from stepping forth and speaking out to help someone in need?

I still have the first Bible I ever owned, a red hardback Bible presented to me at church. I didn't remember who had given it to me until recently when I opened up the front cover to read the words handwritten by my first-grade Sunday school teacher, Mrs. Prouse. The Bible was her gift to me on that Easter Sunday, and exactly three weeks later, she led me in the sinner's prayer to make the Lord my Savior as we knelt together at the altar. Mrs. Prouse, during that one year she poured her life into mine, had no idea I would one day be in ministry. However, she did what she could when she had the chance, blessing me with her love and wisdom.

How could Miriam know that her baby brother drawn from the Nile would be God's man of deliverance for her people? She couldn't, but she acted in loyalty and bravery for her family when she had the chance, stepping forth to speak on behalf of one who could not speak for himself.

THE LADIES' CHOIR (EXODUS 15:1-21)

Miriam and Aaron remained in Egypt under bondage, while Moses fled to Midian as a young man after killing an Egyptian (Exodus 2:11–15). When God called Moses to return to Egypt to deliver his people, many decades had passed. Moses was 80 years old when he stood alongside Aaron, his brother, before Pharaoh.

What an exhilarating time in the life of the Hebrew people! God had shown His mighty hand of power as He poured out plagues upon Pharaoh, then parted the sea to allow them to pass over safely onto dry land. They were inspired by the power of God and moved by His great loving-kindness toward them.

∞ JUST FOR FUN ∞

Which Egyptian plague would have been the scariest for you to experience? How do you handle fear?

In Exodus 15:1–18, Moses and the children of Israel sang a hymn of praise to the Lord. Then Miriam led a movement of praise and worship among the women as they followed her with timbrels and dancing feet to honor God in song.

Could this be the birthplace of women's ministry? Miriam had a presence of leadership among the ladies, and they seem to have instinctively followed her lead as a unit in their worship of the Lord. Miriam's song of praise brought glory to Almighty God. She was not merely celebrating, she was helping everyone to focus on the One worthy of all praise!

The women's movement of praise led by Miriam is a beautiful picture of what ministry among women should look like. The focus is not on womanhood, though we embrace who we are by God's creation. The goal is not fun, though working together for a common goal under the banner of Christ is a thrill to our souls. The approach is not divisive, though we can draw away as a group of women to minister and worship in ways especially suited for females. A women's ministry of any sort will unify women for the common goal of pointing people to Jesus Christ, our Deliverer and Friend.

Personal Reflections

How are you uniting with other Christian women in a bond of love through Christ? What is your goal when you get together? What are you accomplishing for the kingdom of God as you work together?

THE INNER CIRCLE (1 CHRONICLES 6:3; MICAH 6:4)

Miriam was in the inner circle of leadership alongside her brothers Moses and Aaron. She must have inspired many other women of her day! The prophet Micah mentions her name along with Moses and Aaron as leaders sent to the Hebrew people as a gift from God (6:4). The genealogical listing of Levi's family in 1 Chronicles 6, filled with the repetition of the phrase *the sons of*, is interrupted by one listing of *the children of*, as Moses, Aaron, and Miriam are named (v. 3). It's clear that Miriam didn't serve in leadership only as a tagalong behind her brothers, for God has named Miriam in His Word as a woman of godly honor.

Miriam was at the top! Well, almost at the top. For all of the visibility she had on a day-to-day basis, Miriam was not always a part of the action. When God called Moses from out of the burning bush, He named Aaron as the spokesman for Moses in the court of Pharaoh (Exodus 7:1), not Miriam. Aaron supported Moses atop a hill during a battle with the Amalekites (Exodus 17:8–13). He was later named as high priest (Exodus 28:1). Moses and Aaron held the highest roles of leadership in the camp.

If you had been Miriam, would you have been grateful to be used by God in any capacity, appreciative of the load your brothers were willing and called to carry, or just a wee bit jealous of two men who exercised the greatest bulk of authority?

Do you measure your worth in the kingdom of God by how many committees you chair or how frequently you're involved in the various ministry projects of the church? We sometimes feel the temptation to compare our positions and our authority with that of other Christians to determine who is "winning" the race. Why? Because the secular worldview teaches that she with the most people beneath her must surely be at the top of the ladder!

Jesus taught us a different way of measuring our success in His kingdom. He said, *"Whoever desires to become great among you, let him be your servant. And whoever desires to be first among you, let him be your slave—just as the Son of Man did not come to be served, but to serve, and to give His life a ransom for many"* (Matthew 20:26–28). Our ambition as Christian women should not be to achieve a status with others positioned at our feet; instead, it should be to bring more people to the feet of Jesus, the Lord of all.

Personal Reflections

Before God accepts our hand of service to Him, He must first receive from us a willing heart that longs to know Him. Read Psalm 51:16–17. Making the burnt offering was meaningless without the heart that matched the offering. Pray about your attitude toward serving God. Use the prayer below, or pen your own.

Dear Father, I want to be Your willing servant. Teach me to serve You with a willing heart that is motivated by love for You. Give me a new direction in my priorities, God, that knowing You will remain at the forefront of my desires. Create in me a love and appreciation for the spiritual leaders in my life, and not a judgmental spirit of resentment. Amen.

We have no need to compete over positions of authority for the work of God, because God has called each one of us to do a different—not lesser or greater, just different—task for Him. Read 1 Corinthians 12:12–27 and answer the questions below.

Is anyone in the body of Christ less valuable because of her function (vv. 15–17)?

Who has determined your role in the body of Christ (v. 18)?

When your brother or sister in Christ is given a blessing or recognition, what should be your reaction (v. 26)?

A LESSON IN HUMILITY (NUMBERS 12:1-16)

I've learned many a lesson on relationships the hard way from the mistakes I've made communicating with my husband. When we were first married, I occasionally egged on an argument, because I couldn't believe his audacity to walk through the kitchen with mud on his shoes, or I was thoroughly put out with him for chewing so loudly. What he and I had to learn was not to spend hours arguing over tracked mud or noisy eating, because they weren't the real issues; they were just fronts for the larger issues that were really on our minds.

Sometimes it's easier to fuss over side issues than to bring to the table what's really bothering us. We may not want to admit why we're upset, because it would reveal our own smallness and personal weaknesses; thus, many times we're tempted to attack the other person on another level to damage her reputation or do harm in another way. Perhaps that's why Miriam and Aaron stirred up trouble over Moses's new bride. The people would likely not think less of Miriam and Aaron for contending with Moses over his wife if they could defame her in the eyes of the public. But they knew they would look bad if people realized their dispute with Moses was really a matter of jealousy. Thus, they tried to hide behind a veil of trumped up self-righteousness.

When God spoke sternly to Miriam and Aaron, His words indicated He was fully aware of all they had said and done.

FAST FACT
During the Middle Ages, Europeans with leprosy had to wear special clothing and ring bells to alert others of their presence.

We know that God knows all, but Miriam's conversation with God is a great reminder to us that nothing—not even the thoughts and intents of the heart—escapes the notice of the Lord.

Miriam and Aaron intended to tear down Moses for the purpose of building themselves up in the community. Jesus warned, *"And whoever exalts himself will be humbled, and he who humbles himself will be exalted"* (Matthew 23:12). Miriam's sin and punishment would have been public knowledge to everyone, because they were delayed from traveling seven days while she was isolated from the camp because of uncleanness (Leviticus 13:1–6). Her shame evidently made an impression on the community, because Moses reminded the people of her leprosy outbreak while he reiterated various laws in Deuteronomy (24:9).

Miriam died before her people reached the Promised Land, but she played a pivotal role in their journey. As a capable leader fulfilling her holy calling beside Moses, she inspires us to find our place in the family—both the physical family and the family of God—and to be the sister support God has called us to be.

PRAYER MOMENT

Heavenly Father, my desire is to worship You with all of my being. May others be inspired to praise Your holy name because of my heart for worship. Teach me to step into the lives of the people around me who are in need, just as Miriam spoke boldly before an Egyptian princess. Show me, Lord, when I am jealous of others, or where I am petty in my attitude toward others because of deep-seated envy. I want to be content and thriving in whatever role You place me in today. In Jesus's name, amen.

MISS BIRDIE'S SPIRITUAL SECRET

Miss Birdie's death was a heavy blow to our church family. All of us loved Miss Birdie, and we couldn't bear the thought of losing this dear saint. As I prayed for her one day during her final days of illness, I came to a great realization. Miss Birdie was quite possibly the most beloved person of our congregation. Yet, she did not serve on any committees. She rarely spoke in front of the church; she didn't sing in the adult choir; and she didn't serve in a visible leadership role in the organizations of the church. Why did the church love her so fervently? Why were we so brokenhearted at her passing?

Miss Birdie's greatest gift to the church was her love for Jesus, which shone brightly from her face and resonated in the pitch of her voice. She lived a life joyfully surrendered to Jesus. When she left for heaven, we were no longer able to enjoy the company of this dear one who taught us by example to draw closer to God day by day.

Reflect on the impact you're making in your sphere of influence. Are you glowing with the joy of the Lord? What are your motivations to serve Him?

PRAYER & PRAISE JOURNAL

Chapter Four

Naomi:

From Bitter to Blessed

By Edna Ellison

he story of two courageous women, Naomi and her daughter-in-law Ruth, begins in Bethlehem, then takes us to Moab (present-day Jordan), and then returns to Bethlehem, Naomi's hometown. Their story—the Bible's Book of Ruth—was written around 1000 B.C.; yet three thousand years later, these two godly women can give us hope for the future and encouragement in our Christian walk.

Naomi's story begins a few years before she met Ruth:

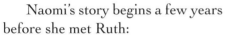

In the days when the judges ruled, there was a famine in the land, and a man from Bethlehem in Judah, together with his wife and two sons, went to live for a while in the country of Moab. The man's name was Elimelech, his wife's name Naomi, and the names of his two sons were Mahlon and Kilion.
—Ruth 1:1–2 NIV

Can you imagine the prayers that went up from this good Jewish family, who believed in Yahweh (Jehovah), the One God? Hungry and probably discouraged, the family moved to the abundant fields in Moab, where they lived for ten years. As the boys grew, they surely made friends with Moabite girls and boys. Then tragedy struck: *"Now Elimelech, Naomi's husband, died, and she was left with her two sons"* (v. 3 NIV). We don't know how old the boys were, but we know times were hard. Mahlon and Kilion eventually married Moabite girls, Ruth and Orpah.

Later tragedy struck again: *"After they had lived there about ten years, both Mahlon and Kilion also died, and Naomi was left without her two sons and her husband"* (vv. 4–5 NIV). The three women remained together, destitute and pretty much hopeless in a world far different from ours. The economic avenues open to women today were nonexistent. And since Naomi was too old to have another husband (v. 12), her only hope was the kindness of strangers.

Fortunately, Ruth and Orpah had a mentoring mother-in-law, a righteous woman who cared for them. She took on five mentoring roles as she poured her life and experience into them. Let's take a look at each of them in turn.

Going Deeper

According to James 1:27, what is your responsibility to widows? Can you think of widows in your sphere of influence who are in need of a caring touch or a helping hand?

SERVANT: HUMBLY HELPING

Despite the seemingly desperate situation, Naomi kept her heart attuned to practical ways to provide the resources her family needed. One of Naomi's admirable qualities was her resourcefulness. She adapted to the situation, whatever it was! When she heard in Moab that God had provided food in Bethlehem, her hometown, Naomi prepared to return to her country. Her daughters-in-law walked alongside her, setting out on the road that would take them to the land of Judah.

In Victorian England, servants catered to the needs of the families, providing resources and caring for others while denying themselves. A *major domo* (Latin, "chief servant") coordinated the other servants. Would you make a good *major domo*? As Naomi provided for her daughters-in-law, how could you serve younger women you know? God may be calling you to mentor as a servant to others who are spiritually hungry. You can lead them to the greatest spiritual resource: the Holy Spirit. What would you be willing to do for your own daughter-in-law? As a godly woman, ask Him to help you have a servant heart.

Naomi could have chosen to abuse her culturally accepted authority, demanding her daughters-in-law wait on her and provide for her. Instead, she humbled herself before them as a servant and shared their fate.

Personal Reflections

Mothers-in-law are often the butt of jokes. But mothers-in-law can have a truly positive and important role in the lives of their children's spouses. What kind of mother-in-law are you (or do you intend to be)?

ENCOURAGER: SHARING A POSITIVE ATTITUDE

How excited the three women must have been when they set out on their journey! Naomi looked toward home; as someone spiritually wiser, she walked alongside the younger women and gave them encouragement. She thanked them for their kindness to their father-in-law and to their husbands. An encouraging mentor, Naomi had given Ruth and Orpah hope, even in their bereavement and grief. She paid them compliments and shared words of encouragement.

Going Deeper

Look at Ruth 1:8–10 for evidence of Naomi's kindness. Could you give your family member well wishes in finding a new husband?

If you had to walk a several days' journey, what would you do to prepare? What opportunities have you been aware of lately, in which God may be moving you into a new area of ministry?

Then Naomi said to her two daughters-in-law, "Go back, each of you, to your mother's home. May the Lord show kindness to you, as you have shown to your dead and to me. May the Lord grant that each of you will find rest in the home of another husband." Then she kissed them and they wept aloud and said to her, "We will go back with you to your people."
—Ruth 1:8–10 NIV

How tenderly she kissed both girls; how sweet were her parting words; how sincere were her tears! She wanted what was best for them, regardless of her own fate. In the end, Orpah tearfully decided to return to her mother's home in Moab, but Ruth insisted on going with her mother-in-law to find a new life in a strange land. Naomi's mentoring of Ruth surely became more intensive as they found a place to live together.

Like today's book agent or talent agent, Naomi promoted her daughter-in-law, hoping for *her* bright future! Naomi sent Ruth to the threshing floor, trusting young Ruth with the responsibility for their only hope and livelihood. Without an encouraging agent, many professionals today would flounder. Ever in the background,

Women of the Covenant

Naomi was an excellent agent, nudging Ruth into the limelight so she could soar! Naomi was an encourager in every sense of the word! Are you an encourager? Listen to God as He speaks to you now. He may be calling you to mentor someone as an encourager.

Counselor: Offering Unselfish Wisdom

Naomi offered wise advice, becoming not only a servant and an encourager, but also a counselor. As a counselor, Naomi unselfishly sought the best for Ruth, regardless of her own needs. Like the Holy Spirit our Wonderful Counselor whispers to us, Naomi whispered wise words to her daughter-in-law. She must have helped her cope with death and discouragement. Slowly the two women became mentor and *merea* ("ma-RAY-ah", a Hebrew word meaning "companion" or "friend") as they bonded spiritually. The words in Ruth 1 show how tender their mentoring relationship was. Ruth loved Naomi, her spiritual mother, and refused to leave her. (Even Orpah had cried tears at the thought of leaving her.) Ruth was able to face the future with courage, with her godly counselor by her side.

Do you remember in *The Sound of Music* when two nuns go to their Mother Superior, saying "Reverend Mother, we have sinned," revealing the distributor caps they'd ripped from the now-disabled Nazi cars in order to allow the Von Trapp family to escape? Each nun knew she had sinned, yet damaging the motors seemed appropriate at the time. As Christian women, we, too, benefit from having a "Reverend Mother"—a more spiritually mature mentor to help us cope with the seemingly gray areas of life as well as the hardships—to listen with a tender ear to our challenges and dilemmas.

And Naomi was a marriage counselor, as well! Ruth met Boaz, and later lay at his feet, as was the Bethlehem custom; Naomi arranged with Boaz to go before the local council, clear Ruth's good name, and establish a proper marriage. Naomi seemed wise in every area of life.

TEACHER: SHARING KNOWLEDGE AND EXPERIENCE

As they journeyed to Bethlehem, Ruth must have spent many evenings listening to her mother-in-law share her knowledge of the local customs. Naomi shared the scope of her experience, detailing what she had learned from the past. Perhaps Ruth learned about Bethlehem life at the same time she memorized the Holy Scriptures from her godly mother-in-law.

Have you been blessed with such a teacher? If so, you have been on the receiving end of his or her talent, ability, and unselfishness. Will you now offer your teaching ability to God? Whatever it is that you know, can you teach it to another woman, enriching her life? Anything! Consider the possibilities: canning tomatoes, typing, praying, mothering—offer your entire scope of knowledge to another . . . for Him.

The most important thing you can teach another woman as you mentor her is how to have a relationship with the Redeemer. Naomi identified Boaz as their *kinsman-redeemer*, a relative who would reclaim lost women—widows, slaves, or the sick—who had no one to provide for them (Ruth 2:20 NIV). Today, though social structure has changed dramatically, we still need someone to provide for us spiritually. We look to Jesus as our Kinsman-Redeemer, our Brother (Hebrews 2:11) who provided a way for God to adopt us as joint heirs in the family of God!

FAST FACT

The Sound of Music was based on a true story. The singing Von Trapps had three children together in addition to the seven stepchildren, and one of them became a missionary to Papua New Guinea.

Women of the Covenant

Personal Reflections

Who do you know who needs to know Jesus as Savior?

How are you allowing God to use you to draw these lost people to Christ?

Make a list of people you know who need Jesus. Begin praying for them regularly.

GUIDE: MODELING THE WAY TO GO

Once you've met the Redeemer, who guides you, claims you as His own, and purifies your heart along the way, you can guide others to open their hearts and let Him in. Instead of loping along with a limp or an awkward gait, you can be confident in Him, a woman who can soar! One mark of your Christian maturity is that you don't let your friends merely lope along when they could be soaring. You pick them up and carry them along. As a mentor, Naomi guided Ruth in many ways: she led her to Israel, modeled how to live in Jewish culture and showed her how a woman of the true God worshipped. Don't you imagine that Ruth spent time every day just watching what Naomi did and then copied her? Like a flea on a dog (no offense intended in the analogy), Ruth went along for the ride, experiencing all that Naomi experienced, growing in wisdom and knowledge.

Think of yourself as that gentle yet sturdy dog. You can ask a *merea* to look at life from your perspective. You can call to her, in effect, "Hop on my back — I know the way." Dog-and-flea mentoring is the easiest way to mentor: just take your *merea* as you go to church, to a women's conference, or to serve at a soup kitchen. Show her how a godly woman follows good paths. As you guide her, you can point her to Jesus, who will lead her through the dark valleys of life.

GET REAL!

Ruth 1:11–13 reveals Naomi's honesty in facing reality. When you're discouraged, do you have a close friend with whom you share? Naomi made herself vulnerable with Ruth and her relatives as they reached Bethlehem (Ruth 1:19–21). She didn't hide her discouragement from her relatives, saying, *"Call me Mara* [a place of bitterness], *because the Almighty has made my life very bitter. I went away full, but the LORD has brought me back empty"* (NIV). As Christian women, we are tempted to wear a plastic smile, pretending our lives are perfect. We have much to learn from Naomi as an example and guide!

How can you be a mentor, like Naomi? She left a legacy of wisdom and experience God used in the lives of others. Her support of Ruth had far-reaching, even eternal, consequences. God multiplied her faithfulness many times over. In Ruth 4, we find Naomi babysitting with Ruth and Boaz's newborn baby, Obed. Ruth became the mother of a royal legacy: Obed was the grandfather of King David, an ancestor of Jesus—our King of kings!

Personal Reflections

Has God given you experience, knowledge, skills, or networking that you could share with a *merea*? To which mentor roles may He be calling you to serve?

How do you "get real" with your church friends or unchurched neighbors? Do you pretend you have all the answers in life, or do you demonstrate real joy amid life's problems?

Have you asked Jesus to become your Redeemer? If not, why not? I pray that you will ask Him to enter your heart as He becomes your Lord in everything.

If Jesus is already your Savior, how has He made a difference in your life? Consider how you can deepen your relationship with Him right now. Write down some action steps you can take to draw near to God.

PRAYER MOMENT

O God, how You have blessed me! I thank You humbly for all the gifts and experiences You have given me, even the hard ones. Help me to use those to help others walk through their dark valleys. Enable me to serve, encourage, counsel, teach, and guide, within Your will and plan for my life. Bring others into my path whom I can help and let me walk alongside them to share Your overflowing love. Purify my heart along the way and keep me alert to holy opportunities to bless them. In the name of our Redeemer, amen.

⤳ Heart Connections ⤥

THE HAPPY WIDOW

After marrying the boy next door (actually two doors down), we settled in the neighborhood and had two children—a girl and a boy. I was proud of my faithful husband, a fervent deacon, and our children, active in missions and youth Bible studies. Our son, Jack, left for college, as our daughter, Patsy, moved to the tenth grade. Jack came home one weekend for a football game, seeming wise beyond his years as he offered advice to his sister, who marched in the band. Life couldn't have been better!

I went to that game a happily married wife and mother and came home a widow. As we watched the game, my husband slumped. In minutes he died of a massive heart attack, in spite of the efforts of doctors and CPR technicians who came quickly from the stands to help.

God keeps His promises! That week He began to fill me with peace that really does pass all understanding. He changed this wimpy, dependent housewife into a happy widow, trusting Him to satisfy all needs.

God enables us as we help others walk through their dark valleys. We can help women navigate through difficult life circumstances because we've been there. My life verse, Romans 8:28, says, *"And we know that in all things God works for the good of those who love him, who have been called according to His purpose* (NIV)." I can encourage a struggling widow, because I have experienced that pain and now testify that God is faithful to be the husband to the widow.

I praise God for what He's still doing in my life, what He's done in yours, and what He will continue to do as He holds you by *"His righteous right hand!"* (Isaiah 41:10 NIV) Begin looking for a woman who may be walking along a path you've been down before and offer to walk alongside her as a friend and mentor along the way.

PRAYER & PRAISE JOURNAL

CHAPTER FIVE

HANNAH:

A BUNDLE OF JOY

By Kimberly Sowell

One morning my precious preschooler bounced down the stairs and said, "Momma, I've been thinking about it, and I think we should watch a movie, go to McDonald's, and then you can take me to the playground. OK?" The twinkle in her eye was hard to resist.

"Oh, Baby, that sounds like a wonderful idea, but unfortunately, Momma has some things she's got to do today."

That precious little one promptly positioned her hand on her hip as she responded, "Well! You have just ruined my plans for the day!"

Most mornings, you and I have an idea of what we think our day should look like. In fact, many of us would admit that since we were little girls, we've had an idea of what our entire *lives* should look like. We have plans, what we believe to be reasonable expectations, but life doesn't always turn out the way we expect it. Does it?

Hannah's name means "grace" in Hebrew, and she had to live out the meaning of her name as a daily act of courage, because her life was not turning out the way she had expected. Hebrew women wanted to have children, and those who couldn't, like Hannah, were looked down upon with shame. How do we cope when life doesn't offer us what we deeply desire?

Longings of the Heart (1 Samuel 1:1-8)

Hannah knew she had the infertility issue and not her husband Elkanah, because he had children by his other wife Peninnah. I remember sitting in my parents' den one afternoon with heaviness of heart, talking with them about the pain that was weighing me down. After several months of tests and medications, the fertility specialist said that nothing more could be done for me. My husband was fine, but I had a problem that could not be corrected, leaving us no hope to conceive. My dad was trying to show compassion, but he couldn't understand why I was immediately thinking about adoption. I kept saying I felt that I *needed* a child. My mother could fully relate and explained, "A woman just knows when it's time."

Elkanah wanted to take away Hannah's sorrow, but he could not comfort the mother's heart of his childless wife. Peninnah could have better related to Hannah's longing, but she tormented her with taunting. Yet Hannah did not lash out in anger. Nonetheless, Hannah's pain was real, and it was deep.

Can you relate to Hannah's sorrow? Maybe you or someone you love has experienced infertility. Or maybe you've longed for a husband, but Prince Charming never showed up. For a woman living for the Lord, desiring a child or a husband doesn't seem like an unreasonable request to make of God, does it? However, God has a specific will for each of our lives, and our plans must bow to His will.

As women living by faith, how do we cope with those times when God does not grant us what we feel we need? In my life, I had to journey with the Lord down a road of soul searching until I realized only God could be the center of my desires—not a child, a husband, a career, an answer to a question, not even a healing or relief from a situation—only in God could my soul be satisfied.

Fast Fact

According to the American Pregnancy Association, infertility affects about 6.1 million people in America.

Women of the Covenant

Going Deeper

What are the three messages of Psalm 16:11? Put each phrase into your own words.

Is your soul satisfied? Is it well with your soul?

RISING WITH CONFIDENCE (1 SAMUEL 1:9-18)

Hannah poured out her soul before the Lord. She didn't carry her burden alone, because she knew she could talk to God about the longings of her heart. As God directed her prayer, she vowed that her son would be given back to the Lord to serve as a Nazirite. Was she bargaining with God? Probably not. Giving away a toddler son (having weaned him as a toddler) would be no less difficult than going through life with no child at all. How amazing that the son she prayed to bear was the answer to the prayer of Israel for a spiritual man to lead the people in righteousness and integrity.

Eli was not on top of his game that day, because he accused a woman deep in prayer of being drunk. Hannah was humble and full of grace toward him, referring to herself as a "maidservant" in her response to him and in her prayer to the Lord. Eli blessed her as she departed, and how remarkable that *"her face was no longer sad"* (v. 18).

Hannah rose with confidence in the trustworthiness of God. Her countenance showed what her heart believed—that God had heard her prayer. *"Now faith is the substance of things hoped for, the evidence of things not seen"* (Hebrews 11:1). Her faith made the impending birth believable; it was a faith so strong she could almost feel the baby boy in her arms.

Personal Reflections

Consider Psalm 42:5: *"Why are you cast down, O my soul? And why are you disquieted within me? Hope in God, for I shall yet praise Him for the help of His countenance."*

Sometimes we say, "I hope so," when we're asked to give our thoughts on the outcome of a problem. Do you have worldly hope—desiring that God will work through the situation but you aren't sure—or do you have godly hope—a confidence in the goodness of God?

What has your countenance been saying about your trust in God lately?

A WOMAN OF HER WORD (1 SAMUEL 1:19-28)

Hannah probably enjoyed about three years of pouring her life into her precious Samuel. He was an answer to prayer, a gift from God, and a child with a great future in service to the Lord. I wonder if Hannah indulged in extra cuddles and extended rocking sessions with her baby boy, knowing her time with him would be short.

My husband and I adopted a baby boy from Guatemala. During the adoption process of waiting and praying, I was able to visit our baby Jay for a weekend. He was mine for two entire days, and every minute was a precious treasure. At the end of the weekend, in the wee hours of the morning before the adoption lawyer would come to take my son away, I fell to the floor and cried out to God. I had stayed up all night watching Jay sleep, realizing I was about to have to give my son away. As I begged God to help me at this moment when I didn't have the strength to let him go, God reminded me of a comforting thought: Jay always had and always would be in the care of his Heavenly Father, and I could trust God to watch over my son.

FAST FACT

Elkanah, her husband, could have revoked Hannah's vow to God if he desired to, according to the law recorded in Numbers 30.

Hannah was able to release her precious son into the arms of God because she trusted Him. She visited Samuel each year with a gift of a little robe (1 Samuel 2:19), and each year she was able to return home without her son.

Look down at your hands. Do you have white knuckles and clenched fists, holding onto someone or something that you love dearly? Are you willing to release that person or that situation into the arms of God?

Personal Reflections

Consider Mary at the foot of the Cross, watching her Son being crucified. Think about Hannah kissing the forehead of little Samuel and then walking away. About what or whom is God calling you to trust Him? What do you need to do?

A Satisfied Soul (1 Samuel 2:1-11)

My sister Carolyn was my playmate growing up, and she and I have remained very close through the years. She lives far away, and we rarely get to visit, but when we do, the ending is always the same. I say my good-byes, and then I have a tearful fit of boohoos.

Hannah was a remarkable woman! She responded to the separation from her son with a song in her heart. *"My heart rejoices in the Lord"* (1 Samuel 2:1). In her own strength, she probably would have melted into a puddle on the floor, but in God's strength, Hannah brought glory to God for His matchless character and might. What a testimony!

First Timothy 6:6 gives us the secret to Hannah's joy:

Now godliness with contentment is great gain. For we brought nothing into this world, and it is certain we can carry nothing out. And having food and clothing, with these we shall be content.

As a follower of Christ, everything we need for godliness and contentment is found in Him. Do you look around and acknowledge that what God has given you is enough?

Hannah's longing was for a child, but what other potential areas of discontent can you think of in your marriage, career, family, church, or in yourself? What has you distracted lately? Are you frustrated over your old couch, or do gray hairs and fallen arches have you feeling down?

∞ JUST FOR FUN ∞

Make a list of things in your house you would like to replace. Compare your list with a friend and see if you can swap some stuff to give both of your homes a new look!

God offers "great gain" to a godly and content heart, but "great gain" may not mean a new sofa or a body overhaul. Most of what we suffer discontent over can fall into the category of stuff, comfort, or pleasure, and Jesus did not die to offer us stuff, comfort, or pleasure. The great gain He offers includes love, peace, joy, righteousness, forgiveness, and eternal treasures in heaven with Him.

Going Deeper

Read James 4:1–7. What kind of damage can an unchecked lust of the flesh cause? How is Hannah the antitype of verse 3?

Read Hebrews 13:5–6. The message is that we can be content with what we have because Jesus is enough. Why do you suppose this passage addresses fear in the midst of a lesson on contentment? When we're discontented, what is our fear?

God delayed giving Hannah what she desired, but we know that God loved Hannah. Her season of infertility surely strengthened her prayer life and taught her to fully rely on God. Perhaps the unique manner in which Samuel was conceived was a testimony to him that God had a special calling on his life from an early age. And in due time, according to God's perfect will, Hannah gave birth to five more children. Hannah was truly a blessed woman, because she had learned to be filled with joy with or without what she felt she must have, realizing that God was her source of joy. Are you drawing from the well of great joy that is Jesus Christ?

PRAYER MOMENT

*Precious Lord, You are enough. Let me dwell on this thought today: You **are** enough. I bring my petitions before You today, and I ask You to help me to release all of my concerns, sorrows, and desires into Your loving arms. I want to say in all truth: it is well with my soul. Teach me to be content. In Jesus's name, amen.*

∽ *Heart Connections* ∾

My Joy

Hannah's story is close to my heart, because I have lived her pain. I have been diagnosed with a disorder affecting my fertility that my doctors cannot explain or repair. I remember during the time of the diagnosing process mourning over the loss of what could have been, realizing that there was nothing I could do to fix my problem. There's a certain hopeless feeling when we realize that something we want so desperately is beyond our control—that no amount of money and no level of personal sacrifice is going to make it happen. But then God stepped into the picture.

One morning I lay on my bed reading Hannah's song (1 Samuel 2:1–10). I was weeping tears of joy, and for the first time, I was able to rejoice alongside her as my sister in the family of God. It was the morning of the day I would go to the doctor to find out if God had opened my womb, and I was reading Hannah's words and feeling grateful that I serve the kind of God who is *able* to open the womb. Knowing that He may not do it for me, I was still overwhelmed with joy that He did it for her, one whose pain ran so deeply into her soul.

That afternoon I found out that God had also *"granted me my petition which I asked of Him"* (1 Samuel 1:27). Months later, I gave birth to a baby girl. Four years later, God once again broke through an unexplained disorder and granted another pregnancy to me. I praise God to the highest heaven in gratitude for all three of my little bundles of joy (precious Jay's coming through adoption is also by the gracious hand of God). And truly I rejoice in a lesson learned: the Lord will always be my source of joy.

PRAYER & PRAISE JOURNAL

CHAPTER SIX

PHOEBE:

A WOMAN GOING PLACES

By Kimberly Sowell

With God's gifting, women have accomplished incredible feats in history. Women from many cultures have shown bravery in battle, wit in literature, leadership in

politics, innovation in science, and let's not fail to mention—patience and poise in the home! God loves and values women. We are special because we are made in His image, and, as Christians, He has declared us worthy through Jesus Christ.

God gives each of us different skills, according to His divine plan for how we might glorify His name in our corners of the world, but what is common to every one of us is a divine calling to minister in the name of Jesus Christ. Whether you're currently spending your days as a plumber, architect, nurse, teacher, office manager, or mommy, your life matters to God. Have you said yes to God's calling in your life?

Personal Reflections

Do you embrace the belief that you're called to minister for Christ? What preconceived notions do you have about what it means to minister?

I commend to you Phoebe our sister, who is a servant of the church in Cenchrea, that you may receive her in the Lord in a manner worthy of the saints, and assist her in whatever business she has need of you; for indeed she has been a helper of many and of myself also.
— Romans 16:1–2

As Paul closed the Book of Romans, he named particular Christian brothers and sisters who were noteworthy to him. Phoebe was among those commended to the Christians in Rome. The Greek word Paul used for *commend* means "to place together." As he introduced Phoebe to the Roman believers who were meeting her for the first time, he wanted to unite their hearts with Phoebe's for God's glory as they would minister together. In view of the stamp of approval Paul presented to the Romans on behalf of Phoebe, he clearly valued her ministry. Not only was she entrusted to deliver this important letter (the Book of Romans) to the believers in Rome, but also Paul had opened the door for whatever other ministry she might be involved in while visiting that city.

Phoebe is a strong New Testament example for women who desire to find their places of service in the kingdom of God. Throughout the New Testament Scripture, we read of women who devoted themselves to ministry in the name of the Savior. Jesus had many female followers who served Him (Matthew 27:55; Luke 8:1–3), and Paul's teachings also elevated women's standing in the family of God. He often mentioned women as great contributors to kingdom work, such as Priscilla (Romans 16:3–4) and Mary (Romans 16:6). Many women are mentioned in The Acts of the Apostles, such as Philip's daughters who were prophetesses (21:9) and Dorcas the benevolent seamstress (9:36).

Fast Fact

The Greek word translated "helper" in Romans 16:2, which describes how Phoebe had benefited Paul and others, means "protectress" or "patroness."

Personal Reflections

Which women in Scripture do you admire the most? Which qualities of theirs do you desire to have in your spiritual character?

Does every Christian woman have a calling to serve the Lord by serving outside of her home in some capacity?

Take to Heart the Importance of Balance

Phoebe's ministry began in her home church in Cenchrea, a harbor town near Corinth. As we serve God within our home church, we exercise our spiritual gifts for the good of that body. Among our church family is a safe and fitting place to learn the ropes of any ministry, to grow in knowledge of God, to strengthen our walk with Christ, and to invite God to sharpen our focus on His calling in our lives.

Phoebe's ministry of helping—helping missionary evangelists like Paul—grew as God called her to serve in ministry beyond her church walls. How amazing that a woman in the early church had a traveling ministry, taking her to Rome! Perhaps you've thought about how God might use you, but dismissed ministry ideas because of the busyness of your season of life. Phoebe, like so many women who serve God in and out of the church, certainly faced difficult choices of priorities and sacrifice, but she was willing to walk through the doors of service for Christ because she loved and trusted Him.

What difficulties do you suppose Phoebe faced in her ministry? If she was anything like the average woman of today, she likely faced a constant battle to stave off guilt and to maintain balance in her life. We ladies can be our own worst enemy when it comes to guilty feelings that weigh us down and pull us into mental gymnastics, causing us to second-guess our every move. For the Christian woman serving at home, serving in the church, and honoring God out in the world, balance is key.

Imagine your life as a sand castle. Have you knelt in the sand at the beach lately to build a towering house fit for a king? Sand castles require balance. If you attempt to build a sand castle using too much water, or conversely if your sand is too dry, neither imbalance will allow the castle to stand. The proper consistency requires a delicate ratio of water and sand. The sand castle also must be built on a solid foundation; otherwise, even the sturdiest structure will easily erode.

FAST FACT

Cenchrea is mentioned one other place in the Bible, Acts 18:18. On his return to Antioch from Corinth, Paul stopped there to have his hair cut off. Some commentators believe this act signaled the beginning of the end to a Nazirite vow Paul had made after either the Macedonian or Corinthian vision. If so, Paul ended his vow in Cenchrea with thanksgiving, acknowledging God's faithfulness in helping him to complete the mission he had been given.

[Source: IVP New Testament Commentaries, http://www .biblegateway.com/resources/ commentaries/]

Your challenge as a woman of God is to balance your life, considering your relationship with God, your relationship with your family, and your self-maintenance. If you neglect your relationship with the Lord, your very being will suffer and you will miss the point of living (Luke 9:25). If you neglect your relationships with family and friends, you miss out on the experiences of life that God offers you as a blessing and a source of strength (Ecclesiastes 4:9–10). If you neglect your self-maintenance by robbing your body of sleep, rest, exercise, learning opportunities, nutrition, and recreation, you rob yourself of opportunities to develop who you are in Christ and will potentially damage the vessel God has given you

Women of the Covenant

(1 Corinthians 6:19). And of course, *no other foundation can anyone lay than that which is laid, which is Jesus Christ* (1 Corinthians 3:11).

Going Deeper

Read Job 29:4–6. Can you identify these three longings of Job's heart?

- Quality time with God

- Quality time with family

- Quality time with himself

When you find your life out of balance, which arena do you typically neglect: God, family and friends, or self?

Is it possible to maintain that balance, thriving in our walk with Christ? As we look at the life of Jesus, the answer is yes. Note that Jesus had an earthly ministry that lasted only about three years, yet He remained in balance as our Savior, fully God and fully man. Jesus never neglected to pull away to be alone and replenish, and we find Him taking time to eat and sleep. Jesus also chose to spend time with His earthly family and friends, even attending a wedding. In addition, Jesus frequently retreated to spend time communicating with His Father in prayer. If Jesus, knowing that His time of earthly ministry was limited, chose to balance His life, we can also strive for balance in every season of life.

Personal Reflections

Jesus knew His ministry on earth would span three years. If you knew you had three years left on earth, how would your lifestyle change?

BE A SISTER, BE A FRIEND

Just as Paul encouraged the early church to bless Phoebe in ministry, we also are able to bless those in our sphere of influence who are serving God in ministry. What are the needs of ministers for Christ, whether they are vocationally serving God or serving unpaid in the church?

Paul asked the Christians in Rome to receive Phoebe as a sister. She was not simply a visiting dignitary, a business associate, or a needy stranger; she was a family member to these believers even though they had never met this sister in Christ. She was worthy to be received graciously because of her unity with them in the Lord.

Those who lead in ministry can feel lonely and isolated from the family of God. Many of them are separated from extended family and feel the void of that support base. Some ministers have to travel extensively, leaving them unable to develop close friendships on a regular basis; while other ministers suffer the loneliness that results from being kept at a distance from others who may feel uncomfortable or intimidated by their presence. Christian ministers have very real, very normal needs that all of us experience, including a need for friends. They need someone to shop with, someone to eat with, someone to invite them to a movie or a ball game—someone to embrace them as a valued friend.

Going Deeper

Read Romans 12:10–13. Apply these verses to name at least seven ways you can bless someone in your life who is serving in ministry.

BE A PARTNER

Not only did Paul ask the Roman believers to receive Phoebe, but he asked that they assist and equip her to fulfill her calling in ministry. One of the keys to the Romans supporting Phoebe would be their openness to recognize and affirm Phoebe's unique calling. Phoebe had a ministry of helping, and she had helped Paul and other Christian leaders. God is incredibly creative in getting the work of the kingdom of God completed by His children. Today we see people coming to Christ through preaching, puppet ministry, nutrition ministry, sports ministry—the opportunities are limitless. Like the Romans, we can also be encouragers to and supporters of others as God nudges us to help them fulfill their ministry.

∞ JUST FOR FUN ∞

Be a blessing! Prayerfully select someone who has blessed you through his or her ministry and find a way to encourage that person with a gift from your heart.

When Paul requested, *"assist her in whatever business she has need of you"* (Romans 16:2), he was asking the Romans to provide for Phoebe's physical needs. Imagine the faith of Phoebe to show up in a new city among people she had never met before, and with a letter of commendation from Paul, hope to have a place to sleep that night, food to eat, and provisions for her journey home to Cenchrea. Paul felt it was a reasonable expectation for the body of Christ to meet the needs of one of the Lord's laborers.

Going Deeper

Read Luke 10:1–8, an account of Jesus sending out the 70 for ministry.

What stands out to you about the instructions Jesus gave to the men He commissioned?

What stands out to you about Jesus's expectations of the people receiving the 70 men?

How can you care for the needs of ministers, both vocational and volunteer, and of missionaries around the world? Here are some possibilities:

- Learn more about their ministry.
- Visit them, whether in the United States or overseas.
- Write an encouraging note or letter.
- Send a care package with some of their favorite foods.
- Contribute financially to their ministry.
- Pray for them, their family, and their work.

Women of the Covenant

In our society, we're trained to leave no stone unturned as we seek opportunities to better ourselves. Jesus has taught us a better way to live, leaving no stone unturned as we seek to promote the kingdom of God (Matthew 6:33). Look around you anew and recognize the Phoebes in your life. How can you encourage other women who are stepping out in faith to serve God? And what about you? Where is God sending you?

PRAYER MOMENT

Lord, I know You have called me to a place of service in the kingdom of God. I want to offer you all that I have, without reservation. Teach me to be courageous for Your glory. Father, please help me be an encourager to my brothers and sisters as they also seek to fulfill Your calling in their lives. In Jesus's name, amen.

~ Heart Connections ~

Tearful Apology

Some days being a woman in seminary felt like being a polar bear in the desert—let's just say that I stood out in the crowd. I generally positioned myself in the front seating area of each classroom, determined to learn as much as I could from my professors and focus on the task at hand.

One day after class, one of the men who sat at the back of the room approached me and asked to talk with me privately. As we pulled aside, he began to speak, and big tears rolled down his cheeks. He said he needed to apologize to me. I was dumbfounded, because I had barely recognized the man as a classmate and had never talked with him before. He explained that he had sat at the back of the room all semester and criticized me for being in the class. He had made assumptions about me and my "agenda" for being at seminary and had made fun of me to his wife and to our classmates. As the semester had progressed, God had done a work in his heart, and this man had realized I was not there to push an agenda but because I wanted to learn how to be a better servant of God. He asked me to forgive him for the things he had said against me, things I had never heard him say. He and I parted ways that day, truly appreciating one another's calling from God.

Each member of the family of God has a role to play. Serving God can be difficult enough as we battle the enemy; let's be allies to one another! Let's bless each other with love and support. May we embrace our calling with courage and joy, and may we encourage our brothers and sisters to fulfill all that God has given them to do. As the writer of the Book of Hebrews urges, *"And let us consider one another in order to stir up love and good works"* (10:24).

PRAYER & PRAISE JOURNAL

Chapter Seven

The Needy Widow:
Like Oil, the Blessing Flowed

By Kimberly Sowell

The older gentleman was shuffling about, looking tired and frantic. His eyes were desperately darting around the parking lot, and it was obvious he had lost something important. I approached him and asked if I could help, and he readily accepted my offer. He had lost his cane, which he evidently had laid aside while he rested his weight on his shopping cart. When we finally spotted his cane in his then-deserted buggy, his eyes filled with joy and his voice was brimming with relief.

I have experienced that same desperate feeling a few times myself. Once I was lost in the middle of nowhere on unmarked country roads after dark. Another time I left my pocketbook at the mall. One time I was late for an important meeting and couldn't get the garage door to open. However, I have never known the depths of desperation that one widow felt when she knew her sons were about to be sold into slavery.

∞ Just for Fun ∞

Describe a time when you felt panicked.
How did the situation resolve itself?

The woman featured in 2 Kings 4:1–7 is unnamed, but we can feel her pain as it jumps off the pages of Scripture. Her story becomes ours as we think about the many times we have been faced with an impossible situation, powerless to solve the issue. What can we learn from this widow? Read her story in its entirety in 2 Kings 4:1–7, then examine how we can exercise our faith as we seek God's hand of provision.

THE OBEDIENCE FACTOR (2 KINGS 4:1–3)

She was down to nothing but a jar of oil, not even enough to make a last meal for her family, but she was not concerned about food; the widow wanted to save her sons from being sold into slavery. The prophet Elisha was the man she turned to in her moment of desperation, knowing that this man of God could guide her through this gut-wrenching trial.

God asked the widow to make preparations for her blessing. Her act of obedience was to go to her neighbors and ask for empty vessels. This was truly a "what will the neighbors think?" moment; she was without food, without any resources, yet she was asking for empty jars. The sensible request might have been for food, or for money to borrow, or livestock to trade, but no, she was to ask for empty vessels. Did the neighbors think she had gone mad over the loss of her husband and the impending loss of her sons?

Sometimes God allows a blessing to flow into our lives through the help of another person. But sometimes He increases our faith by asking us to prepare for a blessing directly from His hands. God could have asked the widow to gather resources from her neighbors, but the beauty of gathering empty vessels lay in the fact that God wanted her to experience a miracle only He could perform.

It's not uncommon for God to require us to take a step of faith. When Joshua led the people to the Promised Land, they had to cross a swollen River Jordan. Joshua told the people that God had promised to part the waters for them to cross safely, but He would do so only *after* the priests who were leading out front had placed their feet in the swelling waters (Joshua 3:8, 13–17). Before we are given the blessing of witnessing His power with our own eyes, we are often asked to take an initial step of faith.

Going Deeper

Is there an act of obedience that God is calling you to take today? Do you need to make a lifestyle adjustment?

The challenge in taking a step of faith is stepping out into the unknown. What does Jesus say about blind faith in John 20:26–29?

In my personal walk with God, I have found that God will wait on me to act in obedience to Him. Once I went through a major transition in my ministry. Early into the process, I sensed God telling my heart to expect something new on the horizon, and I was to prepare myself by letting go of something that was dear to my heart. I delayed because I wanted to hold onto it until I could see what God was going to bring into my life to replace that loss, to fill the void that would come. The more I delayed my obedience, the more frustrated I became about the transition. As I prayed about my uneasiness, it was as if God was saying to me, "We'll sit right here on this square until you're ready to obey." When I finally obeyed the Lord, sweet peace rushed over me. In the midst of our darkest hour, there is peace when we obey the voice of the Lord, navigating us through the storm.

THE FAITH FACTOR (2 KINGS 4:4A)
Don't miss this simple instruction from the Lord—the widow was to go into her home and shut the door behind her. God had spoken to her through Elisha, but she was to make no mistake about the

source of the miracle that would occur in her life. God Himself was going to personally intervene in her hour of need.

Whom do you run to when you have a problem? Elisha was an obvious source of help for the widow, and you probably have some obvious choices, as well. I can always count on my parents, my husband, my church family and friends to step into my situation and lend a helping hand. However, God would have us remember that *"every good gift and every perfect gift is from above, and comes down from the Father of lights, with whom there is no variation or shadow of turning"* (James 1:17). Elisha could only do what God empowered Him to do, and our friends and family cannot solve our problems or answer all of our questions. Only God can supply our every need, and this realization builds our faith in Him.

Going Deeper

Read Philippians 4:19: *"And my God shall supply all your need according to his riches in glory by Christ Jesus."*

Will you memorize this verse to encourage others and yourself when needs arise? How can you use this verse to open a spiritual conversation with someone who is in need?

THE CONTROL FACTOR (2 KINGS 4:4B-5)

The widow had very little to contribute to the solution of her problem, just a jar of oil. But what little she had, God asked her to pour it out. Have you ever noticed that when you pour oil out of a measuring cup into a different container, some of the oil remains in the measuring cup? That's the nature of oil. Pouring the oil into her neighbors' containers would have resulted in a slight loss of her resource every time, if it weren't for the miracle God performed. The Lord was teaching the widow a lesson in complete surrender. Imagine the scene as the widow tipped the jar to begin pouring for the first time. She had to trust God with the only thing she had left, and in doing so, she was giving up complete control of the situation.

Have you surrendered to God in the trials of your life, or are you still trying to wield control over your resources? Remember, your resources include your time, talents, money, and a long list of other things that you may be tempted to think you control. The truth is that none of us control anything. But the Lord can take whatever we offer back to Him—even a sack lunch—and He'll bless it and multiply it into a feast.

Personal Reflections

Write down the heaviest trial or most difficult decision you are facing. Are you attempting to retain control over some portion of the situation?

As you think about your resources, which ones do you find most difficult to surrender into God's complete control?

The Expectation Factor (2 Kings 4:6-7)

Speaking through Elisha, God told the widow to gather up vessels: *"Do not gather just a few"* (v. 3*b*). The house must have brimmed with giddy excitement as the two sons handed their mother vessel after vessel, the widow filling up each one from the same jar of oil. The widow must have been a diligent gatherer of pots, because the measure of oil after God's miracle was enough to pay her debts, save her sons from slavery, and meet her financial needs for the future.

Fast Fact

Slavery is still widespread. The International Labor Organization of the United Nations estimates there are 12.3 million people in forced labor, bonded labor, forced child labor, and sexual servitude at any given time.

[Source: US Department of State Web site, www.state.gov, 2007 figures.]

In a tangible, measurable way, the widow was blessed in accordance with her measure of expectation. The oil did not cease to miraculously flow until she ran out of the vessels that she had gathered in obedience to God's first instruction.

What is your measure of expectation as you approach God for a blessing? Perhaps you have no trouble imagining God blessing your pastor, or your godly mother, or a missionary, but do you struggle to believe that God wants to bless you?

God is an extravagant Giver. Jesus took five loaves and two fish and heartily fed a crowd of 5,000 men plus the women and children—with 12 baskets of food left over (John 6:1–13)! Now that is abundant blessing! Jesus was feeding many men who would very soon turn away from Him and cease to follow Him (John 6:26–27, 60–66). You can believe that God desires to bless you, His precious one!

Going Deeper

What does Jesus teach about persistence and expectation in Luke 11:5–8?

Are you exercising your faith as Jesus instructs in Matthew 7:7–11? According to Jesus, how does the help of an earthly father compare to the provision of our Heavenly Father?

Compare this passage to its parallel passage in Luke 11:9–13, noting the variation in wording in verse 13. Luke placed emphasis on Christ's promise of the Holy Spirit. What role does the Holy Spirit play in giving us good gifts from above?

The old saying, "Desperate times call for desperate measures" is not to be found in Scripture, because our Father has no desire for us to feel desperate. Our stressful mountains become molehills when God's provision intersects with our needs. Our complete surrender to Him is not an act of desperation; it is an act of faith, and our hope in Christ is an anchor to our souls (Hebrews 6:19).

Prayer Moment

Father, I need You to intervene in my problems today. I can't fix what is broken or replenish what has been taken away, and I am fully depending on You to meet my needs. What is the act of obedience You desire of me? How can I get in position to receive Your blessing? Please show me if there is any area in my life I have not fully surrendered to You. Thank You in advance for what You will do, because I know You are a good God. In Jesus's name, amen.

SWEET RELEASE

When it was time for my then infant daughter Julia to take her nap, she would rub her eyes and yawn, but nevertheless fight the sleep she needed by kicking her legs, waving her arms, cooing and singing—anything to keep herself awake. After a while, I would wrap her up into a little ball, and we rocked. She would whine in great protest for a short moment, but when the struggle was over, her precious little frame would go limp and she would close her eyes. This is the moment of sweet release—when we cease to fight what we really needed all along but were too afraid to let go.

Several years ago as I lay in my bed one night praying, God brought to my mind this question: Is there anything in me that is hindering the work of God? Had I hampered the work of the Holy Spirit with any sinful attitude? I opened my Bible and began to read, and the verse God brought to my attention was a warning to avoid focusing on finances and rather to follow God's calling and trust God fully. That was the answer! The truth fell down from heaven in an instant, and I immediately knew what God wanted me to do!

For some time I had sensed God calling me into a women's speaking ministry, but thus far I had found nothing but closed doors. I had planned to continue in my career as a teacher until those doors began to open. I had not even considered quitting my job. After all, how would we pay the bills? God said, "Trust Me." He led me to Hebrews 11:6 that night, which has become a theme verse for my life: *"But without faith it is impossible to please Him, for he who comes to God must believe that He is, and that He is a rewarder of those who diligently seek Him."*

I did quit my job, then went to seminary, and now have the ministry God wanted for me. God is faithful to meet your every need. Whatever you're wrestling with today, may God grant you sweet release.

PRAYER & PRAISE JOURNAL

CHAPTER EIGHT

THE MOTHER OF KING LEMUEL:

A GODLY WIFE

By Edna Ellison

*H*ave you ever received good advice that changed your life? A wise mother, aunt, teacher, or mentor-friend can be a valuable character-shaping influence on any woman's lifestyle. I've been blessed with many mentors and wise advisors all my life. I remember several times I was on the brink of a terrible choice in life when someone nudged me in a different direction. For instance, at an early age, I knew better than to  make certain wrong choices, because my parents wouldn't allow them. Their moral stance protected me. During my teen years, Christian peers helped me stay on track. Later, younger as well as older women gave me valuable advice I could follow. Some of us escape temptation and irresponsible mistakes by vicarious learning experiences: we watch the mistakes of others or read and follow the good advice of others who have experienced failure and warn of the misery it causes.

The most important fact we know about Lemuel, who may have been the king of Massa, is that his mother was a wise woman who gave him good advice, which was saved and recorded. He may have been one of the descendants of Ishmael (the son of Abraham and Hagar, Sarah's servant). Even though Ishmael's tribe were outcasts, they survived—even thrived—in the desert and found a considerably good life, relative to their times. No doubt Lemuel's mother was ahead of her time. She shows extraordinary wisdom that is still applicable for our lives today.

Giving Good Advice

King Lemuel's mother advised him not to spend his strength or time on ungodly women and drinking (Proverbs 31:1–7), but to rule wisely, speak up for those unable to speak for themselves (v. 8), judge fairly, and defend the rights of the poor and needy (v. 9). Then she gave him a list of the desirable qualities of a wife of noble character. We can infer from her words that King Lemuel's mother herself was a godly wife, since she recommended these principles for living.

∞ Just for Fun ∞

What is the worst advice you've ever received?
What is the worst advice you've ever given?

Going Deeper

Read Proverbs 31:10–12. Then answer the following questions.

Why do you think it's hard to find a woman of noble character? How do you think Old Testament lifestyles were different from the typical woman's lifestyle today?

How can a wife bring her husband "good," not "harm"?

Is it significant that verse 12 sets a time frame on a wife's good motives and actions? Why or why not?

We aren't told whether King Lemuel followed his mother's good advice. We assume he did, since this piece of literature was preserved and included in Proverbs, along with wise words collected by Solomon (Proverbs chapters 1 through 29) and Agur (Proverbs 30). Many other biblical passages do contain accounts of people receiving good advice. Solomon received from his father, King David, all the plans and details for building God's temple in Jerusalem (1 Chronicles 28 and 29). Solomon, who loved his father, followed every detail of the plan. He had a successful reign for two reasons: he followed the wisdom of his father David, and he asked for and received wisdom from the Lord and followed His advice (1 Kings 3:9–12). King Lemuel and his mother, along with King Solomon and his father, understood godliness and pointed others to His eternal wisdom, which never fails.

Personal Reflections

Most people have trouble taking advice unless they trust the person giving it. Have you ever had trouble taking your mother's advice? How did you learn to trust her? What about your father?

In the New Testament, Paul tells of two Christians who gave good advice. Priscilla and her husband, Aquila, who had traveled with Paul, stayed in Ephesus, where they met Apollos, a remarkable Jewish evangelist who *"spoke with great fervor and taught about Jesus accurately, though he knew only the baptism of John"* (Acts 18:25 NIV). After hearing him, the couple invited Apollos to their home and *"explained to him the way of God more adequately"* (Acts 18:26 NIV). Though Apollos was obviously gifted (and would later have a popular ministry [1 Corinthians 3:4–9]), he took their advice and then *"was a great help"* to other Christians in Achaia (Acts 18:27–28 NIV).

Going Deeper

If you had been Apollos, would you have followed Priscilla's or Aquila's advice?
Why or why not?

Assuming Lemuel was a young man (say 21), would you have followed his mother's advice at that age?

Do you think peer pressure affects the noble character of women today? If so, in what ways?

Paul advised Christians to follow the advice of other leaders (Stephanas, Fortunatus, and Achaicus, 1 Corinthians 16:17–18). Do you have a good role model whom you trust who demonstrates the qualities of a woman of noble character?

Have you ever grown tired of trying to be a godly woman? Explain:

What is the value of a godly woman remaining consistent in her devotion to God *"all the days of her life"* (Proverbs 31:12)?

WORKING HARD

In Proverbs 31:13–20, the ideal wife performs eight or more activities that indicate she is not lazy or neglecting her family. She gets up early to provide for her family and is active outside as well as inside the home. She is physically fit and careful not to neglect the little things that keep a family going. Like modern women, she has work and hobbies, yet she still finds time to help others.

Going Deeper

List at least eight activities the ideal woman performs in verses 13–20. Do you think she was a good business-woman? Why or why not?

How does she grow physically fit?

According to verse 20, how do we know she was compassionate and missions-minded?

WORKING HARDER: MULTITASKING

Frankly, don't you think the ideal woman in this Scripture works too hard? During a Bible study one Sunday morning, a woman in my class said, "I just hate that Proverbs 31 woman! She worked too hard. She makes all the rest of us look bad! She needed a vacation on the Riviera, or at least, an overnight at a spa."

Tell the truth. Isn't there a little of my friend's attitude in you? I have often wondered what her strong arms (v. 17) looked like. Did she work so hard she

FAST FACT

According to the US Department of Health and Human Services, being physically active can reduce anxiety and may help lower the risk of colon cancer, breast cancer, heart disease, and stroke.

was emaciated? Was she overweight or underweight by today's standards? Have you wondered what the ideal woman's husband was doing while she was multitasking?

My daughter is a schoolteacher, and she gets up before dawn, dresses in the dark, and carpools to school with two other women as the sun comes up. Does getting up early, as the Scripture says, make her more godly than others who begin their work around 9:00 or 10:00 A.M.?

Since parenting has always been a full-time job, who kept the ideal woman's children while she did all these other things?

Personal Reflections

How do these activities of the ideal woman compare to activities in your life?

How do you grow physically fit? Explain how your physical activities are like or different from this woman's activities.

Because you've been blessed like the Proverbs 31 woman, how do you show your compassion and love for others who are not so fortunate?

Are there other things God may be calling you to do now to help others? If so, list them here and pray about what you can do for Him.

RISING BEYOND THE BASICS

Proverbs 31:21–24 shows the abundant life of the man who marries a godly woman and the benefits to his entire household. She alleviates the family's fears by planning ahead for emergencies. Through her sewing and marketing skills she brings respect to her husband in the community.

Going Deeper

Today we live in a world filled with emergencies caused by hurricanes, tornados, earthquakes, floods, upheavals in changing governments, and family crises. How does King Lemuel's mother suggest the ideal woman prepare for emergencies? (v. 21) How does this apply to your life today?

What do you think she does to bring her husband respect?

Do you think the husband or wife is the most influential in beginning and maintaining an exemplary family life?

Personal Reflections

How do you prepare for emergencies in your household?

Which example from this ideal woman's life gives you the best advice for the future? Why?

What kind of respect does her husband seem to have in the community?

How does a woman's reputation influence her husband's respect in *your* neighborhood? How does a man's reputation influence his wife's respect?

Name someone in your neighborhood who has set a good example for other women. What have you learned from her words and her actions?

How can you encourage your husband and children to live "a cut above" the average?

Are material possessions important in bringing respect in your family's life? What is more important than these?

SPIRITUAL WISDOM

Proverbs 31:25–31 ends this chapter with a spiritual application from the life of the ideal woman, as King Lemuel's mother describes her. She has physical strength (v. 25*a*), emotional health (v. 25*b*), intellectual acumen (v. 26*a*), and social influence (v. 26*b*). She doesn't mind hard work and is careful to tend to her household. Her husband praises her, and her children *"arise and call her blessed"* (v. 28 NIV). Though she may have been charming—and she probably was—her primary attribute was spiritual, not physical beauty. She deserved the admiration and praise of others because she feared the Lord.

Going Deeper

How is the ideal woman clothed? (v. 25)

What do these verses tell us about her sense of humor? Why do you think she was able to laugh about the future?

What characterizes her speech? (v. 26)

What do you think it means that she *"does not eat the bread of idleness"* (v. 27 NIV)?

SPIRITUAL EXAMPLES IN TODAY'S WORLD

Two women in my life gave me abundant attention in my childhood. "Mrs. C" was my Sunday School teacher during the elementary grades. She looked at children at eye level, a wonderful gesture, which made me feel special. Most adults patted me on the head, and I resented their messing up my hairdo! They hardly noticed me, moving on to speak to the nearest adult; but Mrs. C was different. Her kind eyes winked as she nodded at me, and she accepted me in every group. For the first time, an adult besides my parents showed a personal interest in me. She once gave me a coin to put in the offering plate since I had lost mine. That one kindness endeared her to me for years.

A second church woman came into my life at two different times. I'll never forget "Miss J," our Sunbeams teacher, who taught me how to set up Jerusalem in a sand box at age five. She gave all the children a missional view of the world we'd never forget. Years later, she helped disciple me as a teenager and young adult.

As an adult, I realized each of these ladies was not physically beautiful. Some might consider them ugly, but they were absolutely beautiful to me—and to all the other little children whose lives they touched. Truly they were clothed with spiritual strength and dignity! Outer beauty is never the watermark of a godly woman. Her inner beauty satisfies the souls of children and others who surround her.

Personal Reflections

How are you clothed with *"strength and dignity"* (v. 25 NIV)?

What do you think *dignity* means?

Do you laugh *with* people or *at* people? How can you laugh without cynicism about situations or disdain for others?

Can others say you are truly a woman who fears the Lord? Why or why not?

How can you become more like the woman described in Proverbs 31?

PRAYER MOMENT

O God, thank You for giving me the example of King Lemuel's mother. Help me to be a godly woman like her, offering good advice to others. Forgive me, Lord, when I become lazy or "zone out," ignoring my responsibilities to my family. Give me strength of mind, body, spirit, and soul, so I can also serve the poor and needy out of the overflow of Your Spirit. Amen.

~ Heart Connections ~

A Mother's Grace

When I was ten, my grandmother gave my mother an heirloom china tea set made before 1900. When we reached our house, my mother asked me to hold it carefully while she unlocked the front door. I replied flippantly, "Oh, I'm not going to drop it!" To show her how agile I was, I began dancing, juggling the small cups back and forth in my hands, then watching with horror as one cup fell and soon, like dominoes, each piece slipped out of my hands and smashed onto the cement porch in hundreds of pieces.

Slowly I picked up a piece, expecting a tongue-lashing. I quickly got a dustpan and broom and swept up all the pieces, as my mother said in a gentle voice, "We can't put them back together again, Edna. Just throw them into the trash can."

"But don't you think we can glue...maybe one or two cups...?"

"I can tell you're sorry. You didn't mean to do it." I expected her to be angry, yell at me, or tell me how bad I was, but she gave me a hug. My mother always spoke softly, believing the best in her children. That night, in her soft-spoken way, she taught me about love, respect, and forgiveness. Grateful for a godly mom, I wanted to grow up like her, clothed in strength and dignity.

PRAYER & PRAISE JOURNAL

CHAPTER NINE

THE GENEROUS WIDOW:
EMBRACING SACRIFICE

By Kimberly Sowell

While visiting my sister Carolyn and her family, my nephew Luke and I became big buddies. He was young, bright-eyed, and eager to please his Aunt Kim. On the last day of my visit, he spent much of the afternoon busily at work in the garage, trying to make a gift for me. He finally appeared, eager to show me the prize he was hiding behind his back. He first gave a disclaimer; his original intention was  to create a jewelry box for me, but somewhere in the process the project had to be scrapped, and the result of Plan B was resting in his palms. With great enthusiasm, Luke then revealed the much-anticipated gift: a necklace. The jewelry was quite unique, because it was made of two-inch blocks of wood, still covered in splotches of spray paint from the lumberyard, and connected with metal hooks and screw-in O-rings. The pride in his eyes was obvious, and I quickly adjusted my look of shock to a look of joy as I placed the "hardware store look" necklace around my neck. His gift, given out of a heart of love and sincerity, turned a rough-hewn woodblock necklace into a beautiful treasure, one that I still have today.

☙ JUST FOR FUN ❧

What is the most unusual gift you've ever been given?
What did you do with it?

When we consider the treasures of God, we realize we have nothing to offer the Lord that compares to His matchless riches. We have nothing to present God that would meet a need of His, for God is in need of nothing. However, our gifts are precious and well received by God when we give them freely as tributes of love and sincerity. What are the gifts you are offering to your King?

Personal Reflections

List ways you are currently blessing God with your gifts of time, talents, financial resources, or other things. In what ways do you see God blessing your giving for His glory?

His Eyes Will See (Mark 12:41-44)

Jesus was standing in the Court of the Women, where 13 chests were located for people to make charitable contributions. According to Alfred Edersheim in *The Temple* (Kregel Publications, 1997), these chests were called "trumpets" because they were narrow at the top and wide at the bottom, shaped like trumpets. Nine of them were designated for specific offerings that were legally due by worshippers. The other four trumpets were for gifts offered voluntarily.

As Jesus sat observing the people dropping their money into the temple treasury, He was noting their manner of giving. As the Son of God, His perspective was unique, for He was looking into the heart of each giver that day. Even the casual observer, like one of the disciples, would have been able to distinguish the rich man from the poor based on general appearances, but Jesus knew exactly how much each person gave, *and* He knew how much each person still possessed after the gift was given!

The Scripture gives no indication that the widow knew Jesus was watching her. In fact, based on His great commendation of her actions, she likely had no interest that anyone in the temple court notice that she placed money into the treasury. Her giving was a private act of devotion between her and God.

What a comfort it is to know that God is not only aware of our gifts to Him, but He knows the circumstances out of which we have given. God knew that she went home penniless that day. Jesus knew why she had chosen to make this great sacrifice, though Scripture doesn't give us that deeply personal insight into the woman's soul. While she would receive no thanks or gratitude from those overseeing the treasury, God was pleased and would bless her, *"for the eyes of the Lord run to and fro throughout the whole earth, to show Himself strong on behalf of those whose heart is loyal to Him"* (2 Chronicles 16:9).

Going Deeper

One Sunday at church my husband gave me a flat look as I stuck my hand in the offering plate to reposition our envelope, turning it face down. Old habits die hard. I learned that practice from my parents. Why do Christians go to great lengths to be discreet in giving?

Read Matthew 6:1–4, then answer the questions below.

Give an example of doing a charitable deed in order to be seen by others.

Why did Jesus call the trumpet blowers hypocrites in verse 2?

Why does our flesh fight against the notion of doing good deeds in secret?

Whose rewards are more valuable, those of other people or those of God?

More than a Token

Do you love chocolate as fervently as I do? Have you ever noticed that it's easy to share candy from your box of chocolates when the container is full, but it somehow becomes painful to share when only a few pieces remain?

Giving can be a greater exercise of faith when you have very little in your possession. Even when added together, the widow's two mites still had very small monetary value. However, the price was indeed great to the widow, because it was *"her whole livelihood"* (Mark 12:44). What an incredible sacrifice!

We have an expression in our culture that's meant to let the giver off the hook if the gift is little or inadequate: "It's the thought that counts." Indeed, the thought or the intention, whether stingy or selfless, is significant. How remarkable that the widow in this story, with nearly nothing, only two coins, gave *both* coins! We wouldn't have blamed her for keeping one coin for herself, knowing she still would've been giving half of her livelihood away, yet she gave it all to the temple treasury. She went to the temple that day intending to offer God more than a token of her affection; she chose to make a tremendous sacrifice.

My daughter and I were recently discussing what it means to be a follower of Christ and to suffer for Jesus. She expressed her willingness to suffer, and then touted her own brush with suffering as a first-grader—the homework was creating such a strain! I quickly corrected her misunderstanding of suffering, but her misperception was not too distant from what many adult Christians consider the threshold of sacrifice they're willing to make for Christ.

The words *suffering* or *sacrifice* take on heightened meaning when we become educated about the high price our brothers and sisters in Christ around the world are paying as a result of their choice to follow Jesus. In the face of discrimination, abuse, job loss, seizure of property, torture, imprisonment, cruelty, and rejection by loved ones these Christians continue to hold to the Lord through the suffering in order to know Him and to make Him known.

Think about the measure of your life and livelihood you have devoted to the cause of Christ. Do your daily choices represent a life surrendered to Jesus, or are you currently offering a mere token of yourself? As God inspires your heart about what it means to die to self, is God calling you to give your life to Him in a greater measure of sacrifice?

Personal Reflections

Imagine the widow rubbing two coins together in the tips of her fingers as she is about to make a choice. One coin? Two coins? Or simply pass by the temple treasury and keep walking?

Is God bringing to your mind something that you need to give back to Him, and are you considering that choice? Record the raw truth of your thoughts on paper. Ask God to help you discern His will for your giving.

WISE INVESTMENTS

In Luke's account of the widow's sacrificial giving, some of the men with Jesus didn't seem to embrace or understand the lesson Jesus wanted to teach them through the widow's two mites. They followed Jesus's remarks with comments of their own, thoughts that were far from the heart of Christ.

> *Then, as some spoke of the temple, how it was adorned with beautiful stones and donations, He said, "These things which you see — the days will come in which not one stone shall be left upon another that shall not be thrown down."*
> —Luke 21:5–6

Some of the men were not impressed with the widow's two mites, but they were enamored with the decorative displays and ornamentation of the temple building. However, Jesus was not impressed with the handiwork of the building and the money that had been donated to build the structure, for the temple was temporal and would soon be destroyed. The money given to buy fancy ornamentation for the building would amount to nothing when the temple was destroyed, but the widow's investment in the kingdom of God was a gift that would last for eternity.

Women of the Covenant

In this scene, the rich men were impressed with themselves, and the disciples of Jesus were impressed with what rich men's offerings could buy. Our modern minds are just as vulnerable to fall for these types of faulty thinking. God would have us impressed with His generosity, never our own. He wants us to be overjoyed with how believers' offerings can be used to build the eternal kingdom of God (His body, the church), not spent on temporary trinkets in buildings that will fade or crumble over time.

Jesus taught, "Do not lay up for yourselves treasures on earth, where moth and rust destroy and where thieves break in and steal; but lay up for yourselves treasures in heaven, where neither moth nor rust destroys and where thieves do not break in and steal. For where your treasure is, there your heart will be also."
—Matthew 6:19–21

Going Deeper

What do the following verses teach about eternal treasures, or treasures in heaven?

- Matthew 13:44

- Matthew 19:21

- Luke 12:33

- 1 Timothy 6:17–19

More Blessed To Give than Receive

Widows were recipients of charity. God instructed His people to protect them, bless them, and provide for their needs (Deuteronomy 16:11; 26:12; 27:19; Isaiah 1:17). The widow in this story is an example of why widows needed assistance, since her livelihood afforded her only two mites to her name that day.

Have you ever been needy? Perhaps you've had financial needs, or maybe you've experienced an illness or a season of life that put you in a position of having to ask for help. For the widow, neediness was a way of life, but she had guarded her heart against a victim mentality. She was not preoccupied with what others should do for her, but had chosen to focus on what she could do to honor God by blessing others. She was not discouraged by her limitations to bless, but was able to look at her meager assets and see a means to give, even through the two mites in her possession.

Fast Fact

Many of the estimated 40 million widows in India, a majority Hindu nation, are poor and oppressed. In some regions, cultural tradition dictates that widows are forbidden to remarry, and they are forced to shave their heads. These widows are often considered a financial drain upon their families and society and are ostracized because even their shadows are considered bad luck.

[Source: Arwa Damon, "Shunned from society, widows flock to city to die," http://www.cnn.com/2007/WORLD/asiapcf/07/05/damon.india.widows/index.html]

Personal Reflections

Are you struggling with a need in your life? How can neediness distract you from serving God and blessing others? How can serving and giving in the midst of your difficulties magnify your testimony of the faithfulness of God?

My mother has taught me many valuable life lessons, but the advice she gave during a low point in my life brought me to a turning point, transitioning me from indulging in sorrow to basking in joy. As I moped about the house with a mind flooded with concerns over my problems, my mother encouraged me to seek ways to bless others. I chose to take that advice. The volunteer opportunities that God brought my way were great times of healing and restoration for me, as God filled the voids in my life with evidence of His goodness.

Have you been blessed by the hand of God? Yes, yes, and yes again! In good times, give generously of yourself and your resources. In trying times, also give generously of yourself and your resources. God is worthy of your deepest affections and your greatest sacrifice.

PRAYER MOMENT

"Your mercy, O LORD, is in the heavens; your faithfulness reaches to the clouds. Your righteousness is like the great mountains; your judgments are a great deep; O LORD, You preserve man and beast. How precious is Your lovingkindness, O God! Therefore the children of men put their trust under the shadow of Your wings. They are abundantly satisfied with the fullness of Your house, and You give them drink from the river of Your pleasures. For with You is the fountain of life; in Your light we see light."
—Psalm 36:5–9

Heart Connections

HUNGRY FOR GOD

In 2004, a pastor in Swaziland used all of his resources to purchase a one-way bus ticket to Tangaat, South Africa. In Tangaat there is a small mission school where I would be teaching evangelism for a week to a group of church lay leaders and a few pastors. The students took three classes a day, and in the evenings they were to rest and study for the next day. Midweek, I learned that this pastor and another student were sleeping on the cement floor in the basement of the mission school, because they had no money for housing. They were eating off a loaf of bread they had purchased together. This pastor had a wife and children in Swaziland who were anxiously awaiting his return, and he and his family were trusting God in superior fashion, for the pastor did not even have the money to purchase his bus fare home.

I asked the Swazi pastor why he had gone to such lengths to attend classes, and his answer was simple: he desired to be the best pastor and follower of Christ he could be, and he sensed God calling him to go to Tangaat to learn. He and his family were praying in faith that God would provide for his needs, and he was willing to sleep on cement and eat a meal of bread with a grateful heart, because he was learning more about God's Word. What an incredible testimony of giving in faith! And what an incredible testimony of what it means to hunger and thirst for righteousness.

How far will God stretch your faith in the coming days? Will you come to Him with palms open toward heaven, willing to return to God a generous portion of what He has so freely given to you?

PRAYER & PRAISE JOURNAL

CHAPTER TEN

RAHAB:

HARLOT TURNED HEROINE

By Kimberly Sowell

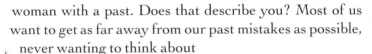

woman with a past. Does that describe you? Most of us want to get as far away from our past mistakes as possible, never wanting to think about or be associated with our former selves. But what if you had to wear the label of your biggest past failure? What if everywhere you went, you were called "Stealing Sally" or "Loudmouth Lying Linda"?

Rahab is remembered as a woman in the lineage of Christ who courageously acted in faith, but she is also associated, to this day, with her unsavory past. As she is named as a positive example for us in Hebrews (11:31) and James (2:25), she is called *"the harlot Rahab"* or *"Rahab the harlot."* Perhaps the tag of *"the harlot"* stayed affixed to her because her life change was so dramatic, and the sharp contrast of who she was against who she became is an inspiring encouragement to all of us. God changes lives. No matter who we are or what we've done, God can use us for His glory, for *"God has chosen the foolish things of the world to put to shame the wise, and God has chosen the weak things of the world to put to shame the things which are mighty"* (1 Corinthians 1:27).

⊗ JUST FOR FUN ⊗

If you had to wear a label for past crimes, what would it be? What about a name reflecting recent changes in your life, like "No Worries Wanda"?

REACTING INSTINCTIVELY (JOSHUA 2:1-7)

God's providential hand led the spies to Rahab, who lived on the wall surrounding Jericho. The men apparently weren't gifted at espionage, because their presence was discovered in no time and was brought to the king's attention. When the king sent instructions to Rahab about the spies in her home, she had to make a split-second decision. She couldn't send the king's messengers away for time to think. She couldn't press the "pause" button on her life to weigh her options. Her quick reaction demonstrated what she valued most (vv. 4–6), and it wasn't self-preservation; a person with no respect for God would have turned over the spies to appease the king.

As a young teenager, I allowed myself to form a nasty habit of using foul language. As I grew in my walk with the Lord and desired to please Him more than anything, I decided to exercise self-discipline and conquer that habit. One day as I turned the corner of my bed, I stubbed my toe on the metal bed frame. Ouch, did that ever smart! As I sat on the bed waiting for the pain to leave, I had a happy thought: I didn't say anything ugly when I stubbed my toe! I uttered a prayer of thanksgiving, because the evidence showed I had turned a corner in my desire for a pure tongue. When I stubbed my toe, whatever was in the forefront of my mind came forth, and praise God, it wasn't trash. My instincts had been transformed by God.

FAST FACT

The Hebrew word translated "harlot" in the Book of Joshua could also be translated "keeper of an inn." However, the Greek word that writers used to describe Rahab in the New Testament definitely means "harlot." [Source: Warren Wiersbe, *The Bible Exposition Commentary*, Old Testament History Volume].

Rahab's heart instinct told her to trust God and protect His people. Jeremiah 8:7 teaches, *"Even the stork in the heavens knows her appointed times; and the turtledove, the swift, and the swallow observe the time of their coming. But My people do not know the judgment of the LORD."* Rahab, however, knew that God's people were going to prevail while the people of Jericho were going to be destroyed for their evil ways. She wanted to be counted among the living, among God's people.

Going Deeper

Read Matthew 24:36–44. How would you describe the world's awareness of the impending judgment of God? Are most people aware? Concerned? Oblivious?

How can you prepare your heart for the coming judgment of the Lord?

DISPLAYING FAITH THROUGH ACTIONS

When the king's messengers arrived at Rahab's door, Rahab risked her life to protect the Hebrew spies. Why? As we read the rest of the saga, we learn that only later did Rahab ask the spies to protect her and her family. She had no reason to expect she would be protected. However, Rahab had a greater hope in the God of Israel. Her protection of the spies was a good work that displayed her faith.

Why do you do good works? As James explained why faith without works is dead, he used Rahab as an example in James 2:25:

"Likewise, was not Rahab the harlot also justified by works when she received the messengers and sent them out another way?" Rahab's act of faith could not have been easy, knowing that her very life was on the line, but her trust in God allowed her to do what was right in His sight. Her faith displayed itself in her actions.

Personal Reflections

When was the last time your faith was tested? What was the good work or action that God called you to do?

A CONFESSION OF FAITH (JOSHUA 2:8-14)

Rahab is blessed among women—she is listed in the genealogy of Jesus Christ (Matthew 1:5)! Consider the connection between Rahab's response to the Hebrew spies and the basic truths of salvation.

We are sinners in need of a Savior. As a person is saved, she realizes her sinfulness, her inability to deal with the problem on her own, and confesses it of God. *"For all have sinned and fall short of the glory of God"* (Romans 3:23). In verse 9, Rahab confesses that *"the Lord has given you the land…and all the inhabitants of the land are faint-hearted because of you."* She knew that Jericho stood guilty before the Lord. She had no doubt that Jericho was defenseless against God, just as we must realize we have no hope of salvation apart from Christ (Acts 4:12).

Jesus is Lord. He is the Son of God, Lord of all. God has revealed Himself to us through nature so that we are without excuse (Romans 1:20), and He speaks directly into our lives. Rahab was an observant woman. She knew how God had revealed Himself through the deliverance of His people and His continued acts of favor (v. 10). Rahab confessed, *"For the LORD your God, He is God in heaven above and on earth beneath"* (2:11). God promises us in Scripture *"that if you confess with your mouth the Lord Jesus and believe in your heart that God has raised Him from the dead, you will be saved. For with the heart one believes unto righteousness, and with the mouth confession is made unto salvation"* (Romans 10:9–10).

"Whoever calls upon the name of the Lord shall be saved" (Romans 10:13). We confess Christ to be our Savior (the One whose blood has paid the price for our sins), and to be our Lord (the One who is God, who is in charge of our lives to lead and direct us). Rahab, after acknowledging who God is and His great authority, asked to be saved from the wrath that God was about to pour out on Jericho (Joshua 2:12–13). She wanted to be numbered among the redeemed, not among the stiff-necked who would not bow the knee to the living God.

Personal Reflections

As you look over the confessions of Rahab and her plea for salvation, have you ever confessed your sins before God and invited Christ to be your Savior and Lord? If you have not, why not trust Him now? Ask Jesus to give you new life and save you from your sins. If you have already turned to Christ, do you have a friend or relative who has not yet made a personal connection with Christ and His power to forgive sins?

Considering Rahab's profession, do you suppose she ever thought she was too far removed from God's love to ask for salvation? What about you?

OBEYING THE TRUTH (JOSHUA 2:15-21)

The scarlet cord was the outward sign of Rahab's decision to be a follower of the one true God. When the Hebrew warriors entered Jericho, they were looking for the cord hung from a window, signifying the one who should be passed over from death.

When God was working through Moses to deliver the Hebrew people out of bondage, the tenth and final plague in Egypt was the death of the firstborn. Moses warned the people the death angel was coming. They were to kill a lamb and spread its crimson blood over the two doorposts and the lintel of their homes so the death angel would know to pass over them (Exodus 12:5–7, 12–13). Rahab's blood-red sign hung from her window, while the Hebrew people's had been spread over their doorposts; perhaps the similarity was striking to some of the warriors as they stormed into Jericho and remembered their people's salvation from the death angel on that night in Egypt.

FAST FACT

Red dyes were produced from vegetables, reddish colored rocks and minerals, and the bodies of insects.

The blood of the Lamb has forever covered our sins, and His name is Jesus Christ. The wrath of God will pass us over on that day when the Lord returns and humanity faces the judgment, because we are covered by the red stains of Christ's blood, which was shed on a wooden cross. As the death angel in Egypt and the warriors in Jericho were looking for the crimson sign, the heavenly Father sees upon us a sign that our sins have been forgiven, washed in the blood of the Lamb, precious Jesus. The Apostle Paul wrote, *"Much more then, having now been justified by His blood, we shall be saved from wrath through Him"* (Romans 5:9).

In Romans 2:7–9, Paul warns of indignation, wrath, tribulation, and anguish for all who reject the truth. At the exodus, the Hebrew people had to obey the truth, believing what God had told them about the death angel and the blood that had to be found on their doorposts. Rahab had to obey the truth, choosing to let the crimson cord hang from her window and to stay within the walls of her home with faith that she would be saved. By hanging out the cord, she was making a statement: "I have chosen to be joined to God's chosen people. I place my full faith in God for my salvation." Jesus said that He is the Truth (John 14:6). We must obey the Truth, and enter into a relationship with God through Jesus Christ. May we live our lives in such a manner that people see that we have placed our full faith in Jesus as Lord.

The tag of "harlot" may have followed Rahab to the New Testament, but she is one of only two women mentioned in the Hebrews 11 hall of faith. Each patriarch and matriarch is heralded as an encourager to us, because each one chose to make pivotal and daring life choices that required faith. It's a life of faith that God finds remarkable and noteworthy. God is calling each of us to display our scarlet cord out of the window of our soul so that others may see and know that we are trusting in the one true God.

PRAYER MOMENT

Dear Lord, I want my life to be a display of Your trustworthiness. I know the blood of Christ was spilled to pay for my sins, and I desire to honor Christ in all I do. Let my transformed life bring You glory forever. In Jesus's name, amen.

CLEAN FROM THE INSIDE OUT

Two days before my sister was born, I returned from Vacation Bible School to find Mother extremely tired. She did a remarkable thing that night: she let me and my brother, Jim, go to bed without a bath. As I jumped into bed, I savored the freedom and settled in...until I noticed grit on my sheets. After playing games in the sandy church yard, my body was covered with a powdery dust; my legs with long, crusty shadows. For the first time, I was *really* dirty!

As I lay there, unable to sleep, I remembered what a minister at Bible school had said: "Edna, you need God." *Yep. So what?* I thought. I had known that since my earliest memories. *Everyone needs God, Creator of the Universe, who provides everything. So what?* Then he said, "And God wants you to be with Him. He wants to use you to share His love with the world." Wow! That hit me right between the eyes...and in my heart. As I squirmed in the gritty bed, I began to remember other things from Bible school: be sorry for my sins, ask God to forgive me, ask Jesus into my heart. For the first time, I knew God—really *knew* Him, feeling His presence all around me in that moonlit room.

I prayed: "Lord, I know You are Almighty; You put the stars in place! I don't understand how You'd want me for anything. I'm skinny, ignorant, dirty inside and out—just a little girl with no power or influence; but right now, I want to give You everything I have. I'm sorry I knocked Jim's tooth out yesterday with that baseball. I'm sorry I pinched Lamar. I'll let him play with us tomorrow and won't pinch him again. I've been mean-hearted this summer, and I don't want to be mean anymore. I want to be clean, inside and out!"

At that moment, God filled me with His Spirit in a powerful way. He and I began a wonderful relationship, and I've never been the same since! I have grown in my understanding and service, but I'll never be able to thank Him for changing me that night. He's become sweeter as the years go by, and I know Him better every day.

—Edna Ellison

PRAYER & PRAISE JOURNAL

Leader's Guide
For Group Study Facilitators

Thank you for choosing to have an impact on the lives of women as you embark on this wonderful journey of Bible study together! Your passion for the Lord, your love of the Scriptures, and your heart for the needs of each woman will shine through each week as you invest in the lives of the ladies who will enjoy this Bible study under your leadership.

Bible Study Features
This Bible study contains elements that will help you as the group facilitator to guide women through the process of engaging the scriptural text of each chapter:

- *Going Deeper*: examines supporting Bible verses that reinforce a scriptural truth found in the chapter. Encourage group participants to look up these additional Scriptures and be prepared to discuss them.
- *Personal Reflections*: invites the reader to make a personal application of a biblical principle. Sharing these, as appropriate, could benefit everyone in the group.
- *Fast Fact*: offers a deeper insight into the text or similar issue.
- *Just for Fun*: provides a lighthearted opening for women to interact with one another on one of the chapter's topics.
- *Prayer Moment*: voices a heart cry to be transformed by the lessons learned from the life of the woman featured in that chapter.

- *Heart Connections*: each chapter ends with a personal story from the spiritual journey of one of the authors.

It is also important that group participants read the Bible story (verses noted in the text's subheads) about each woman featured. Depending on time constraints, you may read the story together as a group or you may ask the women to read each chapter's background story beforehand.

Suggested Format

Each chapter is long enough to fill your meeting time with meaningful truths yet short enough to allow for open discussion among the women. If you desire to cover one chapter per session, consider the following schedule for a one-hour meeting.

10 minutes: Welcome and Prayer

10 minutes: Connect with the Character

30 minutes: Bible Study and Discussion

10 minutes: Closing Reflections and Prayer

What should each of these portions of the schedule look like?

Welcome and Prayer: Thank everyone for coming, make sure that each woman knows the names of others in the group, and welcome new members. Allow the women to share their prayer needs, and pray specifically about their concerns.

Connect with the Character: Help the women to begin connecting with the woman of Scripture featured in that chapter. Consider these suggestions for opening the discussion.

Abigail: *Who is the bravest woman you've ever known?*

Rebekah: *Has your life turned out the way you thought it would?*

Miriam: *Who has been your biggest supporter in life?*

Naomi: *Do you think more people feel bitter or blessed? Why?*

Hannah: *What is your favorite memory of your mother from childhood?*

Phoebe: *How do you know when God is calling you to do something for Him?*

The Needy Widow: *If you were in a severe financial crisis, what is the worst job you would be willing to do to earn money?*

The Mother of King Lemuel: *If you could design a magazine to help women become the ideal woman, what features or sections would you have in each issue?*

The Generous Widow: *Complete this sentence: If God asked me to give _____, I would really feel the pain of that sacrifice.*

Rahab: *How would you describe faith in Christ to someone who had grown up among a people who did not worship God?*

Bible Study and Discussion: Before the session, study the chapter carefully and pray about which points of the lesson you desire to emphasize during your time with the group. You will not have time to delve into every "Going Deeper" question; ask the Holy Spirit to help you determine which questions will most benefit the women as you study together. Decide which of the "Personal Reflections" questions will open the door for meaningful discussion, and which questions are perhaps too personal to ask the ladies to respond to in a group setting.

Closing Reflections and Prayer: As you bring the time of Bible study to a close, you may wish to use the personal story at the end of each chapter to summarize the theme of your Bible study, or share a story from your own life experiences. Invite the women to share one biblical truth that God has revealed to them during your study time together that day.

Encourage the women to read the chapter in its entirety on their own before the next meeting, being sure to complete any questions that you did not cover during your time together. Challenge them to carve out time for careful reflection and prayertime as they ask God to speak to them specifically during their personal study time.

For your closing prayertime, consider allowing the women to pair up. Ask them to share with each other a specific prayer request regarding how they would like to see God move in their lives as a result of what they've learned. You can also pray for the group using the prayer at the end of each chapter.

A Perfect Ending

After you've completed all ten chapters, have a celebration with snacks and party flair! Ask the women to share which of the ten biblical women they related to most and why. Allow them to share what transformations God has brought in their lives through this study. Remind the ladies that being a woman of the covenant means being a woman who has promised her heart to God and has entered into that covenant agreement with God through the means He has provided, Jesus Christ.

LEADER'S NOTES

LEADER'S NOTES

If you've been blessed by this book, we would like to hear your story. The publisher and author welcome your comments and suggestions at: newhopereader@wmu.org

New Hope® Publishers is a division of WMU®, an international organization that challenges Christian believers to understand and be radically involved in God's mission. For more information about WMU, go to www.wmu.com. More information about New Hope books may be found at www.newhopepublishers.com. New Hope books may be purchased at your local bookstore.

Also from

New Hope

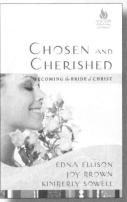

Chosen and Cherished
Becoming the Bride of Christ
Edna Ellison, Joy Brown, and
Kimberly Sowell
ISBN-10: 1-59669-271-5
ISBN-13: 978-1-59669-271-8

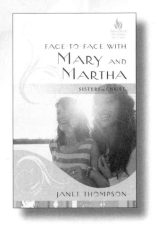

Face-to-Face with Mary and Martha
Sisters in Christ
Janet Thompson
ISBN 10: 1-59669-254-5
ISBN 13: 978-1-59669-254-1

Face-to-Face with Naomi and Ruth
Together for the Journey
Janet Thompson
ISBN 10: 1-59669-253-7
ISBN 13: 978-1-59669-253-4

Available in bookstores everywhere

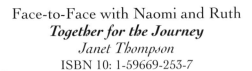

For information about these books or any New Hope product,
visit www.newhopepublishers.com.